Dinner Time

I dedicate this book to my incredible mother, without whom none of this would be possible. Mummy, I'm not always the best at saying it, but I love you, and I'm so grateful to God for you. If I go on to become even half the woman you are, I'll have achieved something truly monumental.

And Daddy, Esther and Oluwadara – thank you for being my biggest supporters. I love you.

Dinner Time

Zena Kamgaing

Photography by Yuki Sugiura

BLOOMSBURY PUBLISHING
LONDON · OXFORD · NEW YORK · NEW DELHI · SYDNEY

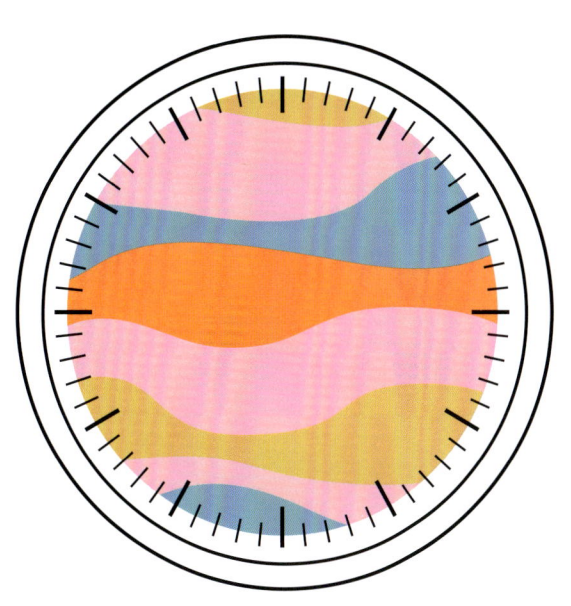

Contents

Flavour Forward

This is your book for easy, big-flavour recipes for busy weeknights, lazy weekends and everything in between – because life can be full on and we all deserve a mouthwatering meal at the end of the day. It's structured around time, because I find that time is one of the biggest things we have to consider when deciding what to cook. Some days we need something quick and easy. Others, we've got the hours (and headspace) to slow down and savour the process as much as the end result.

Wherever you are on that spectrum, *Dinner Time* has you covered. The book is divided into five chapters: 15 Minutes, 30 Minutes, 45 Minutes, 60 Minutes or More, and Sweet Treats. Each chapter offers something different, but they all work towards the same goal: big, exciting flavours, made simple.

I've always been obsessed with big, bold flavours. It started at home, growing up in southwest London in a Nigerian-Cameroonian household. The food my mum cooked was delicious, full of depth and unapologetically seasoned. Flavour came first, always.

Beyond a few staples like red stew (lovingly reinvented on page 156), jollof rice (page 162), and plantain, we didn't eat a huge amount of traditional West African food, but all our meals were deeply flavourful. Onion, garlic, ginger, thyme, curry powder, smoked paprika, cayenne pepper, Maggi seasoning cubes, soy sauce – these were the foundations of my mum's cooking. While they aren't all central to the way I cook now, her love for big, bold flavours certainly is.

As flavour driven as I am in my cooking, I care just as much about whether it fits into the reality of everyday life. And that's precisely what's inspired me to write this book: to show that deeply delicious food doesn't need to be stressful, complicated or take hours to make.

The 15-minute chapter is full of fast, flavour-driven dinners that prove that great food doesn't have to take for ever. The 30-minute recipes give you a little more room to build depth, but they're still quick enough to feel doable after a long day. With 45 minutes, you can unlock deeper flavours and create meals that are more complex but still uncompromisingly easy. The 60+ chapter is all about letting time do the work. And finally, Sweet Treats is full of some of the most delicious desserts you'll ever make – if I do say so myself! The same time frames apply here too, so whether you're after a quick 15-minute pudding or a lazy bake, there's something for you.

I've poured my heart and soul into this book. These recipes reflect my background, my love for global flavours and, above all, my belief that big-flavour cooking doesn't have to be complicated. You can make and enjoy deeply delicious meals no matter how much time you have on your hands.

So, whether you're a confident cook or just starting out, cooking for yourself after a busy day or making a feast for friends and family at the weekend, I hope this book helps make dinner time more exciting. I hope it's something you can turn to day in, day out – no matter how much time you have, the mood you're in, or the energy you've got. Most of all, I hope it helps you find joy in cooking, knowing that regardless of what your day looks like, good food is always within reach.

Happy cooking!

Zena x

Pantry staples

Chinese Flavours

If you love Chinese food, there are a few ingredients that are, in my opinion, absolute must-haves for your pantry. They're long-lasting, endlessly versatile and feature in lots of the recipes in this book (and beyond!), so they definitely won't go to waste.

Light soy sauce: Salty and savoury, light soy sauce is used for seasoning rather than for colour.

Dark soy sauce: Thicker, richer, slightly sweeter and less salty than light soy sauce, dark soy sauce is more for colour and depth.

Oyster sauce: Thick, glossy and full of umami, oyster sauce adds instant depth to stir-fries, sauces and marinades.

Hoisin sauce: Sweet, salty, and fragrant with Chinese five-spice powder (see below), hoisin is great in glazes, dipping sauces and dressings.

Toasted sesame oil: Nutty and aromatic, a little toasted sesame oil goes a long way. It's best used at the end of cooking to bring everything together.

Shaoxing wine: A Chinese cooking wine that adds subtle depth and complexity, Shaoxing wine is great in sauces, braises and marinades. If you can't find it, dry sherry works well in a pinch.

Rice vinegar: See right.

Sichuan peppercorns: Floral, citrusy and numbing, these peppercorns are what give Sichuan dishes that unmistakable tingling heat.

Five-spice powder: A warming blend of star anise, cloves, fennel, cinnamon and Sichuan peppercorns, five-spice is best used in small amounts, to add background warmth to your dishes.

Chinese-style chilli oil: This is spicy, punchy and full of flavour. Some brands are fiery, others lean more towards aromatic – find one that suits your palate and keep it within arm's reach!

My go-to brand for most of these ingredients is Lee Kum Kee – the flavour is consistent and reliable and the ingredient lists are much cleaner than some of the supermarket own-brand versions.

Japanese Flavours

Japanese food has always held a special place in my life. One of my closest childhood friends was Japanese and her mum was an incredible cook. So was she, to be fair! By the age of 17, she was running a successful Japanese food blog and by the time she'd turned 19, she'd self-published her very own cookbook. Some of the recipes in this book are inspired by dishes she taught me. If you love Japanese flavours, here are a few key ingredients worth having in your pantry.

White miso paste: Mild, savoury and slightly sweet, white miso is a key base for soups, dressings, glazes and marinades.

Mirin: A sweet rice wine, mirin is great at balancing out saltier flavours.

Cooking sake: Light and dry, cooking sake is used to tenderise protein and round out savoury dishes. (Note that it is different from drinking sake, which tends to have a higher alcohol content and doesn't contain the small amount of salt that is usually in the cooking version.)

Rice vinegar: Delicate but sharp, rice vinegar is great for seasoning rice, pickling vegetables or giving a lift to dressings. You may see it sold as rice wine vinegar, which is the same thing.

Dashi powder: An easy shortcut to instant umami depth, dashi powder is essential in noodle broths, simmered dishes and soups.

Korean Flavours

I didn't grow up eating much Korean food – my love for it came later. It actually all started with K-dramas. The food always looked incredible: bubbling stews, crispy fried chicken, late-night ramyeon slurped straight from the pot. I'd watch an episode and find myself craving dishes I'd never even tasted.

That curiosity turned into a bit of a fixation, and now Korean ingredients have a permanent place in my kitchen – especially gochujang, which you'll see features in my recipes a lot. If you're looking to explore and incorporate some Korean flavours into your cooking, here are a few pantry staples worth having on hand.

Gochujang: A fermented Korean red pepper paste, gochujang is spicy, thick, sticky and a little sweet, with a deep, savoury backbone.

Gochugaru: Korean red pepper flakes with a warm, smoky heat, gochugaru is what gives kimchi (see below) its signature kick. Gochugaru is brilliant in stews and sauces, or simply sprinkled over other dishes to finish.

Toasted sesame seeds: Simple but essential. I use toasted sesame seeds to finish rice bowls, salads or steamed vegetables – really anything that needs a final bit of crunch and flavour. You can buy them ready-toasted, but it's easy to toast your own by briefly heating them in a dry pan over a medium heat (take care not to let them burn – tip them straight on to a plate once they're toasty).

Kimchi: Fermented vegetables – usually cabbage or radish – kimchi is packed with heat, acidity and umami. Eat it straight from the jar, stir it through rice or use it as the base for soups and stews. Note that if you are vegetarian or vegan, traditional kimchi contains fish sauce – there are, though, many vegan versions widely available these days. Just do check the label to be sure before you buy.

Most of these ingredients are now easy to find in larger supermarkets, but if you can pick them up from a Korean or East Asian grocer, all to the good! The quality and flavour are usually better.

Global Pantry Staples

So many of the recipes in this book are inspired by flavours not just from Asia but from around the world. These are the other pantry ingredients that I come back to time and again. Some of them are bold and punchy, others more subtle – but they all bring something special to the table.

Harissa: A North African chilli paste made with dried red peppers, garlic and spices, harissa is spicy, smoky and a little sweet – it's great in marinades, dressings and stews. My go-to brand is Belazu's Rose Harissa Paste.

Chipotle: Smoked, dried jalapeños, chipotle usually comes as a paste or in flake form. It's rich and earthy, and adds a deep, smoky heat to sauces, soups and marinades.

Thai red curry paste: Your Thai red curry paste should be spicy, bold and aromatic – but not all curry pastes are created equal. Look for a brand that uses real ingredients – Mae Ploy and Thai Taste are both solid options.

Ras el hanout: Warm, aromatic, slightly floral, and one of my favourite ever spice blends, ras el hanout roughly translates to 'head of the shop', implying it combines the finest spices a seller has to offer.

Kecap manis (ketjap manis): An Indonesian sweet soy sauce, kecap manis is thick, glossy and rich with molasses.

Tamarind paste: Sharp, tangy and slightly fruity, tamarind paste adds brightness and complexity to everything from curries to dressings.

Fresh curry leaves: Fragrant and slightly citrusy in flavour, fresh curry leaves are used in South Indian cooking to bring depth to dals, curries and tempered oil blends.

Saffron: Known for its intense colour and unmistakable aroma, saffron is hand-picked from the stigma of a variety of crocus flower. A few strands soaked in hot water or stock will give dishes a deep golden hue and a subtle, savoury richness.

A few cook's notes

Reading the Recipes

I've written these recipes with easy, weekday dinnertime in mind – and that means that there are some ingredients you just don't need to be too prescriptive about. Here are a few top tips for reading the recipes without stress.

Sugar: When I list 'sugar', I mean regular white granulated sugar. But, unless a recipe specifies otherwise, you can usually swap in caster, light brown or dark brown sugar if that's what you have to hand.

Neutral oil: Extra virgin olive oil is the oil I cook with most, but it doesn't always work. Sometimes its flavour is too strong, or it isn't just right for the specific cooking technique (for example, I'd never deep-fry with it). In those cases, I call for a neutral oil – one without a pronounced flavour – such as vegetable, sunflower, rapeseed or avocado oil. Avoid oils like extra virgin olive or coconut oil here, as their flavours can be overpowering.

Butter: Unless salted or unsalted butter is specified in the recipe, either is fine – just keep tasting for seasoning (see below) and adjust as needed.

Salt and pepper: I've never been a salt-and-pepper-only gal (give me all the seasonings), but that doesn't mean that salt and pepper don't have their place in making food delicious (especially roast chicken; see page 160). Do always keep salt and pepper to hand when you're cooking. I've listed them in the ingredients only when calling for a specific quantity. For general seasoning (a pinch here and there to taste), I always use fine sea salt and freshly ground black pepper.

Perfect Rice in 15 Minutes

Rice is such a staple in my home. If you're short on time – or simply don't want another pot to wash up – there are some fantastic microwave options.

I always have at least four Tilda Sticky Rice packets stashed in my pantry for when I want perfectly fluffy sushi rice in under 2 minutes.

Still, cooking rice from scratch is much easier than you'd think. This method is my go-to. It's simple, consistent and works beautifully with both white basmati and jasmine rice (sushi rice can be a bit trickier and varies a lot from brand to brand, so I'd recommend following the package instructions when it comes to cooking that).

For four people: Rinse 250g of rice under cold water using a sieve or a colander, then drain it and tip it into a medium saucepan. Add 360ml of water and bring the water to a simmer over a medium-high heat. Once the water is simmering, turn the heat down to low, cover the pan with a tight-fitting lid and cook the rice undisturbed for 12 minutes, until the water has been absorbed and the grains are tender. Take the pan off the heat and leave the rice to sit, covered, for 3 minutes, then fluff it up with a fork, and serve.

PS: If you're a rice-lover like me, a rice cooker is well worth the investment. I've used the Yum Asia Sakura for years and it delivers perfect rice – of any variety – every single time.

How to Devein Prawns

There are some kitchen tasks that I find oddly satisfying – like slicing onions or chopping herbs. Deveining prawns isn't one such task, which is why I most often buy those that are pre-deveined. This is where a good fishmonger comes in handy – they'll often do it for you and, if you're lucky, throw in the heads and shells for free (perfect for making a delicious stock!).

That said, deveining prawns is easy once you know how. All you need is a small, sharp knife. Simply run it along the back of the prawn to expose the dark vein (which is actually the digestive tract), then tease it out with the tip of the knife or your fingers.

15 Minutes

I love food, and I love the act of cooking even more – the chopping, the stirring, the layering of flavours... all of it. But there are times when even I don't want to spend ages in the kitchen, especially after a long day. Whether you've come home late or are just not in the mood for a lengthy cook, these are the dishes to turn to: fast, flavour-driven dinners that categorically prove that great food doesn't have to take for ever.

All the recipes in this chapter are built on clever shortcuts. There are fast-cooking proteins like fish, prawns, beans and steak, as well as flavour heavy-hitters like harissa, gochujang and chipotle paste – umami powerhouse ingredients that are instantly big and bold in a dish. A lot of these recipes start and finish in the same pan, or they come together with barely any cooking at all. They are joyful, inspirational recipes for when time is short, but you still want something deeply delicious for dinner.

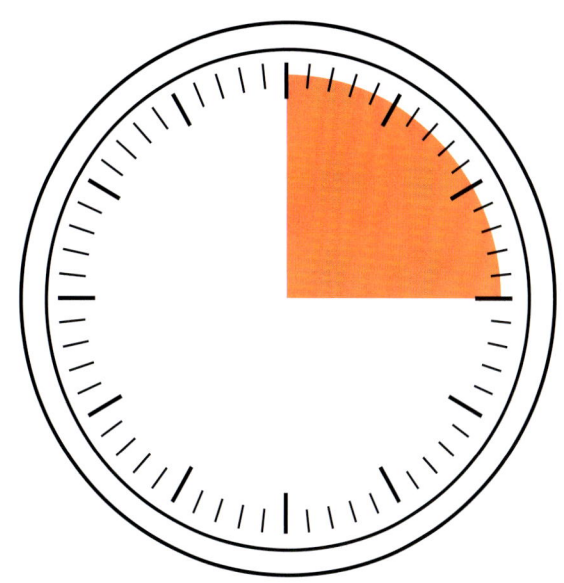

In this chapter

Creamy Tomato & Harissa Pasta

Serves 5–6

500g dried pasta of choice
  (I like a long shape for this)
250g mascarpone
200g oil-packed sundried
  tomatoes (drained weight)
50g parmigiano
  reggiano, grated
25g fresh basil
2 heaped tbsp rose
  harissa paste
1 large garlic clove,
  roughly chopped

This was my first viral recipe, amassing over 15 million views – which, to this day, blows my mind. It was part of my *No-Cook Pasta* recipe series, although I perhaps should've called it *No-Cook Pasta Sauce*, because the pasta obviously requires cooking. Nonetheless, the sauce doesn't, and the whole dish comes together in minutes.

The sundried tomatoes and harissa bring so much depth of flavour, while the mascarpone makes it creamy and rich. It's everything I want in a pasta dish – satisfying, comforting and full of flavour – and it takes next to no effort.

1 Boil the pasta in plenty of salted water according to the package instructions, until al dente.

2 Meanwhile, place the mascarpone, sundried tomatoes, parmigiano reggiano, basil, harissa paste, garlic and 120ml of cold water in a food processor. Season lightly with salt and pepper and blitz to form a chunky sauce. Set aside while the pasta finishes cooking.

3 Drain the cooked pasta, reserving a few ladlefuls of the cooking water, and transfer the pasta back into the pot.

4 Add the sauce with a ladleful of the reserved cooking water and toss until the sauce nicely coats the pasta. Add more pasta water as needed. Divide the pasta between your serving bowls and serve immediately.

Curry Butter Prawns

Serves 4

60g butter
30g double-concentrate
  tomato purée
1 tsp curry powder (mild,
  medium or hot)
2 garlic cloves, finely grated
  or minced
500g deveined raw king
  prawns, tail on
60ml boiling water
1 small handful of fresh
  coriander, leaves and stems
  roughly chopped
Lemon wedges, to
  serve (optional)

Rich, buttery and outrageously delicious, this is the kind of dish that makes weeknight cooking feel effortless. Juicy prawns are tossed in a velvety sauce spiked with curry spices, garlic and the deep sweetness of tomato purée. It's indulgent, easy and perfect with rice, crusty bread or simply on its own.

*Hosting a dinner party? Use **head-on, shelled king prawns** for extra flavour and a show-stopping presentation!*

1 Heat a large frying pan over a medium heat. Add the butter and cook, stirring occasionally, until it just begins to foam and brown (2–3 minutes). You'll notice the sound shift from loud bubbling to a quiet sizzle.

2 Add the tomato purée and cook, stirring frequently, until it begins to darken (2–3 minutes).

3 Add the curry powder and garlic and cook, stirring constantly, for 1 minute, then add the prawns and toss them to coat them in the sauce. Pour in the boiling water, stir and cover the pan. Let the prawns steam until cooked through (4–5 minutes).

4 Remove the pan from the heat and stir in the coriander. Transfer the prawns to a shallow bowl and serve immediately, with some lemon wedges on the side, if you like.

5-Minute Chilli Garlic Tofu

Serves 2

125g white jasmine rice or
250g packet of microwavable
sushi rice
2 tbsp toasted sesame oil
2 tsp toasted sesame seeds
2 tsp gochugaru (Korean
chilli flakes) or ½ tsp regular
chilli flakes
2 tsp sugar
2 tsp light soy sauce
1 garlic clove, finely grated
or minced
1 spring onion, very
thinly sliced
300g silken tofu

This is one of those dishes that comes together in minutes but tastes like you put in *way* more effort. Soft silken tofu is draped in a garlicky sesame sauce that seeps into every nook and cranny. Piled over hot rice, it's one of my favourite quick and easy dinners.

If you'd prefer to serve the tofu warm, you can steam it, poach it in boiling water or microwave it in 30-second bursts until just heated through before adding the sauce. Personally, I love it cold, especially in the summer.

1   If you're cooking the rice from scratch, rinse it under cold water using a sieve or colander, then drain it well and tip it into a pot. Add 180ml of cold water and bring it to a simmer over a medium–high heat. Once simmering, cover the pot with a tight-fitting lid, turn the heat down to low and cook the rice for 12 minutes, until the water has been absorbed and the grains are tender. Take the pot off the heat and let the rice sit, covered, for 3 minutes, then fluff it up with a fork. If you're using microwave packet rice, which I recommend here, heat it up just before serving.

2   In a small bowl, combine the sesame oil, sesame seeds, gochugaru, sugar, soy sauce, garlic and spring onion.

3   Drain the tofu and place it in a shallow bowl. To help the sauce seep in, lightly score the surface with a knife or simply break up the tofu with a spoon for a more rustic feel.

4   Pour the sauce over the tofu and serve with the hot rice (or as it is).

Juicy Tomato Noodles

Serves 2

200g ripe cherry vine
  tomatoes, halved
1 large garlic clove, finely
  grated or minced
1 tbsp oyster sauce (or hoisin
  for a vegan alternative)
1 tbsp light soy sauce
1 tsp rice vinegar
1–2 tsp sugar, to taste
  (depending on how sweet
  your tomatoes are)
1 tsp toasted sesame oil
½ tsp fine sea salt
200g dried noodles (ideally
  thin wheat noodles)
1 spring onion, thinly sliced,
  whites and greens separated
Chilli oil, for drizzling (optional)

When it's too hot to cook and I want something easy, this is what I make – juicy marinated tomatoes with bouncy, saucy noodles. It's fresh, savoury, a little sweet and *just* the right amount of tangy. All you have to do is halve some tomatoes, boil your noodles and toss everything together. The marinade does all the work, drawing out the tomatoes' juices to create a delicious sauce.

To speed things up, place the cherry tomatoes in a single layer between two plates, then press down gently and slice them horizontally through the middle with a serrated knife. It's a quick way to halve loads in one go.

1 Place the cherry tomatoes, garlic, oyster sauce, soy sauce, rice vinegar, sugar, sesame oil and salt in a large mixing bowl. Toss to coat the tomatoes and leave them to marinate for 10 minutes – this will both season the tomatoes and draw out their juices, creating a sauce for the noodles.

2 Meanwhile, boil the noodles in plenty of salted water according to the package instructions. Drain, rinse under cold water and drain again.

3 Add the noodles and spring-onion whites to the marinated tomatoes. Toss everything together, ensuring the noodles are well coated – using your hands is the best way to do this!

4 Divide the noodles between two serving bowls, top with the spring-onion greens and serve. If you'd like some heat, a drizzle of chilli oil wouldn't go amiss.

Buttery Soy Sea Bass with Garlicky Pak Choi

Serves 4

250g white jasmine rice
    or 500g packet of
    microwavable sushi rice
500g pak choi
2 tbsp kecap manis
1 tbsp melted butter
4 skin-on sea bass fillets
    (or sea bream fillets)
1 tbsp vegetable oil, plus more
    for greasing
4 large garlic cloves, finely
    grated or minced

The beauty of this recipe lies in how easily it all comes together. The glaze couldn't be simpler – just kecap manis and butter – but it gives the sea bass a rich, caramelised finish that's salty, sweet and deeply savoury. Meanwhile, the pak choi steams and stir-fries all in one pan with plenty of garlic. Served with rice, this is quick, simple and full of flavour – exactly what you want from a 15-minute dinner.

*If you prefer, **swap in salmon or trout fillets** for the sea bass – just allow a little more time (around 6–8 minutes in total), or cook until the tops are caramelised and the fish flakes easily with a fork.*

1 If you're cooking the rice from scratch, rinse it under cold water using a sieve or colander, then drain it well and tip it into a pot. Add 360ml of cold water and bring it to a simmer over a medium–high heat. Once simmering, cover the pot with a tight-fitting lid, turn the heat down to low and cook the rice for 12 minutes, until the water has been absorbed and the grains are tender. Take the pot off the heat and let the rice sit, covered, for 3 minutes, then fluff it up with a fork. If you're using microwave packet rice, which I recommend here, heat it up just before serving.

2 Meanwhile, heat your grill to high. Line a medium baking tray with foil and oil it lightly. Trim the base of the pak choi to separate the leaves. Wash them thoroughly – really get in there – and drain them in a colander. In a small bowl, mix 1 tablespoon of the kecap manis with the melted butter and a pinch of salt.

3 Pat the fish fillets dry and lay them skin-side down on the prepared tray. Spread the kecap manis butter evenly over the flesh. Grill the fish for 4–5 minutes, or until caramelised and cooked through.

4 Meanwhile, heat the tablespoon of vegetable oil in a large wok or frying pan over a high heat. Add the garlic, drained pak choi and remaining kecap manis. Toss it all together, cover with a lid and reduce the heat to medium. Cook, stirring occasionally, for around 2 minutes, or until the pak choi is tender but still vibrant. Season to taste with salt and pepper, then transfer to a bowl.

5 Serve the fish with the garlicky pak choi, plus the rice on the side to soak up all those delicious, savoury juices.

Steamed Garlic Prawns & Noodles

Serves 2

2 garlic cloves, finely grated or minced
1 tbsp light soy sauce
1 tbsp oyster sauce
1 tsp toasted sesame oil
1 tsp Shaoxing wine
1 tsp sugar
1 tsp cornflour, dissolved in 1 tbsp water
300g fresh egg noodles (from the supermarket fridge section)
165g deveined, peeled raw king prawns
1 spring onion, thinly sliced
Chilli oil, for drizzling (optional)

This is my take on 蒜蓉粉丝蒸虾 (Steamed Garlic Shrimp with Vermicelli), a classic Cantonese dish often served at special occasions. The original calls for big, shell-on prawns and mung bean noodles, but I wanted to create a version that delivers the same punchy flavours in just 15 minutes, using standard supermarket ingredients.

Here, egg noodles and prawns are tossed in a garlicky, umami-rich sauce, then steamed until the prawns are juicy and plump and the noodles have absorbed all that flavour – perfect for a quick but flavourful weeknight meal.

1 If you have a steamer, skip to the next step. If not, place a heatproof rack or upturned bowl in a large-lidded saucepan and pour in enough boiling water to come three-quarters of the way up the rack or bowl. Cover the pan and set it over a high heat.

2 In a small bowl, mix the garlic, soy sauce, oyster sauce, sesame oil, Shaoxing wine, sugar and cornflour slurry until fully combined.

3 Place the noodles in a wide, shallow bowl or platter that fits inside your steamer. Pour over two-thirds of the sauce and toss to coat. Add the prawns to the remaining sauce and toss again.

4 Arrange the prawns in a single layer over the noodles, then carefully lower the bowl into the steamer. If needed, top up with more boiling water so that it still reaches three-quarters of the way up the rack or bowl.

5 Cover the pot with a lid, reduce the heat to medium–high and steam for 8–10 minutes, or until the prawns are opaque and cooked through and the noodles are heated.

6 Remove the bowl from the steamer, top with the spring onion and finish with an optional drizzle of chilli oil. Serve immediately.

Gochujang Pork Lettuce Wraps

Serves 4

Vegetable oil (or any
  neutral oil)
500g pork mince (at least
  10% fat)
4 garlic cloves, finely grated
  or minced
2 tbsp gochujang
1 tbsp light soy sauce
2 tsp sugar

To serve

2 little gem lettuces,
  leaves separated
2–3 spring onions, thinly sliced
1 small handful of fresh
  coriander, leaves and tender
  stems finely chopped
Lime wedges

Spicy, sticky, crunchy, fresh – these lettuce wraps are everything I want in a quick dinner. The pork gets beautifully caramelised, ready to bundle into little gem leaves with lots of lime and fresh herbs. It's bold, bright and *very* delicious. If you're especially hungry, serve the wraps with a side of sushi rice.

Feel free to **switch up the protein** *– beef, lamb and chicken mince and grated extra-firm tofu all take on the glaze beautifully.*

1 Heat a splash of the oil in a large wok or non-stick sauté pan over a high heat. Add the pork mince, breaking it up with a wooden spoon, and stir-fry until the water evaporates and the mince starts to brown (5–7 minutes).

2 Stir in the garlic and cook for 1 minute, then add the gochujang, soy sauce and sugar. Cook, stirring occasionally, for 2–3 minutes, or until the mixture begins to caramelise. Remove the wok from the heat and transfer the pork to a serving dish.

3 Serve the pork with lettuce leaves, spring onions, coriander and lime wedges for easy DIY lettuce wraps.

Dashi Poached Salmon

Serves 2

125g white jasmine rice or
   250g packet of microwavable
   sushi rice
150ml dashi
2 tbsp light soy sauce
2 tbsp mirin
2 tbsp cooking sake
½ onion, very thinly sliced
2 salmon fillets (with or without
   skin, as you prefer)
1 spring onion, thinly sliced,
   to serve

Gyudon – rice topped with thinly sliced beef and onion simmered in a sweet dashi broth – is one of my favourite dishes. This recipe is a pescatarian take on it, and it's even quicker to make because the salmon doesn't need slicing. Served over steaming, hot rice, it's one of the most comforting bowls of food you'll ever eat.

Cooking sake *brings a specific depth that helps round out a dish, but in a pinch, you could substitute it with dry sherry or Shaoxing wine, or omit it entirely if you prefer cooking without alcohol.*

1 If you're cooking the rice from scratch, rinse it under cold water using a sieve or colander, then drain it well and tip it into a pot. Add 180ml of cold water and bring it to a simmer over a medium–high heat. Once simmering, cover the pot with a tight-fitting lid, turn the heat down to low and cook the rice for 12 minutes, until the water has been absorbed and the grains are tender. Take the pot off the heat and let the rice sit, covered, for 3 minutes, then fluff it up with a fork. If you're using microwave packet rice, which I recommend here, heat it up just before serving.

2 In a small saucepan, combine the dashi, soy sauce, mirin and sake. Add the onion, stirring to separate the slices, then nestle the salmon fillets into the broth.

3 Set the saucepan over a medium heat. Once the broth begins to simmer, reduce the heat to low, cover with the lid and cook for 2–5 minutes, depending on the thickness of the salmon fillets, or until just cooked through.

4 Serve the salmon and broth over steaming hot rice, and topped with the spring onion.

Charred Corn & Kimchi Fried Rice

Serves 4

1 × 200g tin of
sweetcorn, drained
1 tbsp vegetable oil (or any
neutral oil), plus more for
frying the eggs
500g packet of microwavable
sushi rice (squeeze the
pouch to separate the grains
before opening)
200g drained kimchi,
roughly chopped
½ tsp rice vinegar (optional, if
your kimchi isn't very sour)
1 tbsp gochujang
1 tbsp light soy sauce
2 tsp toasted sesame oil
2 spring onions, thinly sliced
4 large eggs (optional)
1 tbsp toasted sesame seeds,
for sprinkling
Toasted seaweed, cut into
strips (optional)

Sweetcorn meets spicy kimchi in this flavour-packed fried rice. Charring the corn intensifies it, adding little pops of smoky sweetness that work perfectly with the sour, punchy kimchi. This dish is quick, satisfying and exactly the kind of thing I crave when I want big flavour without much effort. You can enjoy it as it is, with toasted seaweed or topped with a fried egg.

*Traditionally, **kimchi** contains fish sauce, so if you want to make this recipe vegetarian or vegan, be sure to use a suitable version, which will be widely available in supermarkets these days. A fermented, sour kimchi works best, but if your kimchi isn't very sour, add ½ teaspoon of rice vinegar for some extra tang.*

1 Heat a large non-stick wok or sauté pan over a high heat until smoking.

2 Add the sweetcorn and spread it out in an even layer. Cook the corn, undisturbed, for 1 minute, then stir, spread it back out and cook, again undisturbed, for another 1 minute. Stir again, then add ½ tablespoon of the vegetable oil and let it heat for 1 minute.

3 Add the rice and stir-fry for 3 minutes, then transfer the charred corn and rice to a bowl.

4 Heat the remaining ½ tablespoon of vegetable oil in the wok or pan over a high heat. Add the kimchi and cook, stirring occasionally, for 1 minute, then add the gochujang and soy sauce, stirring until everything is well incorporated.

5 Return the corn and rice to the wok and stir to coat them in the kimchi mixture. Spread the mixture into an even layer and cook, undisturbed, for 1–2 minutes, or until the rice crisps up slightly on the underside. Add the sesame oil and the spring onions and give the rice a final stir before removing the wok from the heat.

6 If you're serving with fried eggs, heat a splash of vegetable oil in a frying pan over a medium heat. Crack in the eggs and cook until the whites are set and the edges are crispy, leaving the yolks runny.

7 To serve, divide the rice mixture between four serving bowls and sprinkle with toasted sesame seeds. Enjoy just as it is, or topped with a fried egg and/or toasted seaweed.

Triple Sesame Noodles with Cucumber & Chicken

Serves 4

400g ready-to-wok or
heat-to-eat udon noodles,
or ideally 4 portions of
frozen udon
2 tbsp toasted sesame seeds
2 tbsp toasted sesame oil
2 tbsp good-quality tahini
(see note, page 90)
2 tbsp light soy sauce
1 tbsp rice vinegar
2 tsp sugar
1 garlic clove, finely grated
or minced
400g leftover or cooked
chicken, shredded
1 cucumber, deseeded and
thinly sliced
2 spring onions, finely sliced
(reserve some greens
for garnish)
Chilli oil, for drizzling (optional)

Some dishes are made for hot weather, and this is one of them. The noodles need nothing more than a quick soak, the dressing comes together in seconds and everything is served cold, making it perfect for those days when turning on the hob is the last thing you want to do. The simple but brilliant triple sesame dressing has tahini for body, oil for depth and seeds for texture. Make this once and I guarantee it'll earn a permanent spot in your summer rotation.

*If you can get your hands on **frozen udon**, do! Their texture is unbeatable – so chewy and bouncy – and they cook in just 1 minute. They're increasingly easy to find. Most Asian supermarkets stock them, and, if you have access to a superstore or major city, some of the big-name supermarkets carry them as well.*

***For a plant-based alternative**, swap the chicken for marinated tofu pieces, cooked according to the package instructions. **For a pescatarian option**, serve alongside some seared tuna.*

1 Prepare the noodles according to the package instructions – most just need a quick soak in boiling water – then rinse them under cold water and drain well.

2 Meanwhile, in a large bowl, whisk together the sesame seeds, sesame oil, tahini, soy sauce, rice vinegar, sugar, garlic and 2 tablespoons of water until smooth.

3 Add the drained noodles, along with the chicken and cucumber. Add the spring onions (except for the reserved greens) to the bowl. Season lightly with salt, then toss everything together until well coated. Taste and adjust the seasoning, if needed.

4 Top with the reserved spring-onion greens, and serve drizzled with chilli oil (if using).

Speedy Chipotle Chicken Quesadillas

Serves 2

3 tbsp shop-bought fresh
    tomato salsa (from the fridge
    section), plus more to serve
1 tbsp chipotle paste
120g leftover roast chicken (or
    cooked chicken), shredded
2 large flour tortillas
100g grated cheddar and
    mozzarella blend
Vegetable oil (or any
    neutral oil)
½ lime, juice

These quesadillas are exactly what a quick weeknight dinner should be: bold, flavourful and fuss-free. My trick here is using fresh, shop-bought tomato salsa. You get lots of great flavour from the tomatoes, onions, garlic and herbs, with none of the chopping. The chipotle brings smokiness and subtle heat, while a squeeze of lime at the end adds some much-needed brightness. Served crisp, golden and hot from the pan, these quesadillas truly are the perfect midweek meal.

Instead of the chicken, feel free to use leftover beef, lamb or pork; or, for a pescatarian option, tinned tuna works really nicely. If you're keeping things meat-free, try black beans or cannellini beans – just make sure they're well seasoned with salt and pepper (plus any extra seasonings you fancy).

1 In a medium bowl, mix the salsa and chipotle paste until well-combined, then add the chicken and season lightly with salt and pepper. Mix to combine.

2 Spoon half of the filling on to one side of each tortilla, then sprinkle over the cheese. Fold each tortilla in half, gently pressing down to flatten. Lightly brush the tops with oil.

3 Heat a large non-stick frying pan over a medium heat. Add the quesadillas, oil-side down, and cook for 3–4 minutes, or until crisp and golden. Lightly brush the top with oil, then carefully flip the quesadillas and cook for another 3–4 minutes, or until golden and the cheese has melted. (You may need to cook one quesadilla at a time, depending on the size of your pan.)

4 Squeeze the lime juice into the leftover salsa (it really brightens it up!) and serve it alongside the hot quesadillas.

Crispy Za'atar Sea Bass with Jewelled Giant Couscous

Serves 4

For the giant couscous

200g giant couscous
2 tbsp extra-virgin olive oil
2 tsp harissa paste
1 tsp runny honey
½ lemon, juice
1 garlic clove, finely grated
  or minced
½ red sweet-pointed (romano)
  pepper (or regular red
  pepper), deseeded and
  finely diced
100g baby cucumber,
  finely diced
100g pomegranate seeds
1 small handful of fresh flat-leaf
  parsley, leaves and tender
  stems finely chopped

For the sea bass

4 skin-on sea bass fillets
1 tbsp za'atar
Vegetable oil (or any neutral
  oil), for frying

This is my favourite way to cook sea bass fillets – seared in a hot pan until the skin is perfectly crisp. The seasoning is simple: just za'atar, and salt and pepper, which bring warmth, savouriness and a little complexity without overpowering the fish. You could serve the fish with almost anything, but here I've paired it with a vibrant giant couscous salad, packed with fresh vegetables and tossed in a lemony harissa dressing.

1 Boil the giant couscous in generously salted water according to the package instructions, until tender. Drain, rinse under cold water, then drain again.

2 Meanwhile, in a large bowl, whisk together the olive oil, harissa paste, honey, lemon juice and garlic. Add the red pepper, cucumber, pomegranate seeds and parsley, then season with salt and pepper and toss to combine. Tip in the drained couscous, toss everything together again and season with more salt and pepper, to taste, if needed. Set aside.

3 Pat the sea bass fillets dry with kitchen paper. Season the flesh side with the za'atar, plus a little salt and pepper. Flip and pat the skin dry again, then season lightly with salt.

4 Heat a large non-stick frying pan over a medium–high heat and add a thin layer of vegetable oil. Once hot, place the fillets skin-side down. Press down gently with a spatula for the first 15 seconds to stop the skin curling. Cook the fish for 2–3 minutes, or until the skin is golden and crispy, then flip and cook for 1 minute, until cooked through.

5 To serve, divide the giant couscous salad between four serving plates or shallow bowls. Top each with a portion of the crispy sea bass, skin-side up, and serve immediately.

Harissa Butter Steak Flatbreads

Serves 4

150g Greek yoghurt
2 garlic cloves, finely grated
  or minced
1 small red onion, thinly sliced
1 lemon, juice
4 vine tomatoes (about 300g),
  cut into wedges
2 tbsp extra-virgin olive oil
4 minute or thin-cut steaks
Vegetable oil (or any
  neutral oil)
1 heaped tbsp butter
½ tbsp harissa paste
4 small flatbreads
1 small handful of fresh flat-leaf
  parsley, leaves and tender
  stems chopped

These flatbreads are proof that big-flavour cooking doesn't have to mean long cooking times. Thin-cut steaks cook in seconds, and the harissa butter they're basted in does all the heavy lifting in the flavour department. Nestled on top of warm flatbreads with garlicky yoghurt and a bright tomato and onion salad, they make for a truly delicious and comforting meal.

1 In a small bowl, mix the Greek yoghurt with the garlic and a pinch of salt. Set aside.

2 In another bowl, scrunch the red onion with the lemon juice and a good pinch of salt until softened, then add the tomatoes and olive oil, toss to combine, and set aside.

3 Heat a large non-stick frying pan over a high heat. Pat the steaks dry with kitchen paper, then lightly oil them and season them with salt and pepper. Cook for 1 minute in total, flipping halfway through.

4 Lower the heat to medium and add the butter and harissa. Tilt the pan and spoon the melted harissa butter over the steaks, basting for 30 seconds, then transfer them to a plate to rest for 5 minutes.

5 Meanwhile, warm the flatbreads according to the package instructions. Slice the rested steaks.

6 Spread the garlicky yoghurt over the warm flatbreads, then layer on the steak slices and spoon over the buttery harissa drippings from the pan. Scatter over some of the tomato and onion salad, serving the rest on the side, and finish with a sprinkle of parsley.

Sticky Tamarind Salmon with Roasted Longstem Broccoli

Serves 4

250g white jasmine rice
   or 500g packet of
   microwavable sushi rice
330g longstem broccoli
2 tbsp extra-virgin olive oil
1 ½ tsp chilli flakes
3–4 tbsp sugar
2 tbsp fish sauce
2 tbsp tamarind paste
2 garlic cloves, finely grated
   or minced
Vegetable oil (or any
   neutral oil)
4 salmon fillets

If you've never cooked with tamarind before, this is your sign to start. It's sharp, tangy and zingy, and it's well worth adding to your storecupboard arsenal. Here, it's mixed with fish sauce, sugar and garlic to make a sticky, savoury-sweet glaze that coats the salmon beautifully. Paired with rice and roasted longstem broccoli, it makes for a very delicious, well-balanced dinner.

I'm roasting the broccoli in an air fryer to keep the cooking times as low as possible, but it's of course totally doable in an oven instead – just allow for an extra 5–7 minutes of cooking time.

1   If you're cooking the rice from scratch, rinse it under cold water using a sieve or colander, then drain it well and tip it into a pot. Add 360ml of water and bring it to a simmer over a medium–high heat. Once simmering, cover the pot with a tight-fitting lid, turn the heat down to low and cook the rice for 12 minutes, until the water has been absorbed and the grains are tender. Take the pot off the heat and let the rice sit, covered, for 3 minutes, then fluff it up with a fork. If you're using microwave packet rice, which I recommend here, heat it up just before serving.

2   Meanwhile, heat your air fryer to 180°C. Trim the broccoli and split any thicker stalks lengthways so they all cook evenly.

3   Toss the broccoli with the olive oil, ½ teaspoon chilli flakes and a good pinch of salt and pepper. Transfer the broccoli to the air-fryer basket, making sure not to overcrowd it, and air-fry for 5–6 minutes, or until the broccoli is tender and slightly charred.

4   In a small bowl, combine the sugar, fish sauce, tamarind paste, remaining chilli flakes, garlic and 100ml of cold water.

5   Heat a teaspoon or two of vegetable oil in a non-stick frying pan over a medium–high heat. Place the salmon fillets skin-side down and cook for 3 minutes, or until browned. Flip and cook for another minute, then turn each fillet on to one side and cook for 1 minute. Repeat for the other side.

6   Pour in the tamarind sauce and let it bubble away, basting the salmon as the sauce thickens. After 2–3 minutes, the sauce should be glossy and clinging to the fillets. Serve the salmon with the broccoli and a side of rice to catch every last drop of that sauce.

Silky Crab Linguine

Serves 2

250g fresh linguine (or
  fresh spaghetti)
2 tbsp extra-virgin olive oil
2 garlic cloves, finely grated
  or minced
2 tsp harissa paste
50ml white wine
50g good-quality brown
  crab meat
100g good-quality white
  crab meat
1 tbsp finely chopped fresh
  flat-leaf parsley leaves
Squeeze of lemon juice, plus
  more if needed

Cooking is my love language, and this is how I show someone I care – in just 15 minutes. You've got fresh pasta, buttery crab and a silky, savoury sauce. It's the perfect date-night dish – special and impressive but incredibly simple to make. Or just make it for yourself, because why not?

1 Boil the linguine in plenty of salted water according to the package instructions, then drain, reserving 3–4 ladlefuls of the cooking water.

2 Place the olive oil, garlic and harissa paste in a sauté pan or pot large enough to hold all the pasta later. Set it over a medium heat and let everything sizzle gently for 1–2 minutes, or until fragrant.

3 Turn the heat up to high and add the white wine. Let it bubble for 30 seconds to emulsify, then take the pan off the heat and add the brown crab meat. Season with salt and pepper. Use a wooden spoon or spatula to mash the brown crab meat into the oil and wine, forming a thick sauce.

4 Return the pan to a low heat. Add the drained linguine and a good splash of the reserved pasta water. Toss to coat, stirring vigorously and adding more pasta water as needed until the sauce clings to the linguine and has a glossy, smooth texture.

5 Add the white crab meat, parsley and a good squeeze of lemon juice, then toss to combine until warmed through. Taste and adjust with more lemon or with salt, if needed, then plate up and serve.

No-Cook Prawn & Avocado Tacos

Serves 4

½ red onion, thinly sliced
1 orange, juice
2 limes, 1 juiced, 1 cut into
  wedges to serve
300g cooked, ready-to-eat
  king prawns
1 red chilli, thinly
  sliced (optional)
1 large avocado, stoned
  and peeled
1 small handful of fresh
  coriander, leaves and tender
  stems finely chopped
8–12 soft taco shells (if you
  can find corn ones, they're
  the best!)

This recipe has summer running through every delicious mouthful. You simply toss ready-to-eat prawns in a zingy citrus marinade, then pile them on to warm tortillas with a quick avocado salsa. There's no actual cooking involved, just a bit of chopping and mixing. The result is bright, fresh and unbelievably easy – exactly what you need on a hot summer's night.

1 In a medium bowl, scrunch the red onion with the orange and lime juices and a good pinch of salt until it begins to soften. Add the prawns and red chilli (if using) and toss to combine, then season with salt and pepper. Refrigerate for 5 minutes.

2 In a small bowl, mash the avocado, then strain in the citrusy prawn marinade. Season with salt and pepper, and mix to combine – this is your avocado salsa.

3 Toss the now drained prawns and onion with the coriander.

4 Warm the tortillas according to the package instructions, then it's time to assemble. Spread a little avocado salsa on to each tortilla, top with the marinated prawns and serve with lime wedges. Alternatively, serve everything DIY-style – prawns and avocado salsa in separate bowls and warmed tortillas on a plate for everyone to help themselves.

Tomato & Egg Stir-Fry

Serves 4

250g white jasmine rice
  or 500g packet of
  microwavable sushi rice
Vegetable oil (or any
  neutral oil)
2 spring onions, thinly sliced,
  whites and greens separated
400g vine tomatoes, cut
  into eighths
1 heaped tbsp oyster sauce
1 tsp sugar
4 large eggs
1 tsp Shaoxing wine
1 tsp toasted sesame oil

Few dishes deliver on simplicity and flavour quite like this quick Chinese stir-fry. Sweet, savoury and incredibly comforting, it's a midweek lifesaver that comes together in under 15 minutes and is perfect with hot rice.

If you're vegetarian or allergic to oysters, use hoisin or soy sauce instead of the oyster sauce. The flavour profile will be different, but the dish will still be delicious!

1 If you're cooking the rice from scratch, rinse it under cold water using a sieve or colander, then drain it well and tip it into a pot. Add 360ml of cold water and bring it to a simmer over a medium–high heat. Once simmering, cover the pot with a tight-fitting lid, turn the heat down to low and cook the rice for 12 minutes, until the water has been absorbed and the grains are tender. Take the pot off the heat and let the rice sit, covered, for 3 minutes, then fluff it up with a fork. If you're using microwave packet rice, which I recommend here, heat it up just before serving.

2 Meanwhile, heat a splash of vegetable oil in a large non-stick frying pan, wok or sauté pan over a medium–high heat. Add the spring-onion whites and stir-fry for 30 seconds. Add the tomatoes, oyster sauce and sugar. Stir to combine, cover and cook for 3 minutes.

3 While the tomatoes are cooking, whisk the eggs with the Shaoxing wine and a generous pinch of salt and pepper.

4 Remove the lid from the pan and continue to cook the tomatoes, stirring occasionally, for another 3–4 minutes, or until they become thickened and jammy.

5 Push the jammy tomatoes to one side of the pan and pour the egg mixture into the empty space. Cover and cook for 1 minute to let the eggs set, then remove the lid and gently scramble. Once the eggs are almost cooked, mix them into the tomatoes until fully combined.

6 Remove the pan from the heat and stir in the spring-onion greens and toasted sesame oil. Serve immediately with hot rice.

Peanut Butter Gyoza Noodles

Serves 2

150g dried soba noodles (or any thin noodles)
8–10 frozen gyoza (depending how hungry you are)
2 tbsp natural smooth peanut butter
1 tbsp light soy sauce
1 tbsp rice vinegar
2 tsp sugar
1 tsp toasted sesame oil
1 garlic clove, finely grated or minced
2 tbsp hot water
½ cucumber, cut into matchsticks
Optional toppings: chopped or picked fresh coriander, roasted peanuts and chilli oil

This is what I make when I've got gyoza (or any dumplings, really) in the freezer and no energy to cook, but I still want a deeply delicious dinner. The base is cold soba noodles tossed in a perfectly balanced peanut sauce – sharp, salty, nutty and a little sweet all at once. As for the dumplings, the possibilities are endless, and you can cook them in whatever way suits you best. I like to steam-fry mine, but if even that feels like too much, you can simply boil or microwave them instead. The cucumber adds crunch and freshness, and if you've got some coriander or spring onions kicking about, you can throw them in there too.

1   Boil the noodles in salted water according to the package instructions, then drain, and rinse them under cold water.

2   Cook the gyoza according to the package instructions – whether that's steamed, steam-fried, boiled or microwaved, time it so they're ready just as the noodles are done.

3   Meanwhile, in a large bowl, whisk together the peanut butter, soy sauce, rice vinegar, sugar, sesame oil and garlic with the hot water until smooth. Add the drained noodles and toss until well coated. Taste and adjust with a little more soy or vinegar, if needed.

4   Divide the noodles equally between two serving bowls. Top with the gyoza and cucumber, then scatter over the coriander and peanuts, if using. Finish with a drizzle of your favourite chilli oil, if you like.

Turkish Eggs, But Italian

Serves 2

200g ricotta
1 small garlic clove, finely
    grated or minced
3 tbsp butter
1 tsp double-concentrate
    tomato purée
¼–½ tsp chilli flakes
4 large eggs
Fresh basil leaves, to
    garnish (optional)
Crusty bread or toast, to serve

Breakfast for dinner is a regular occurrence at my house (we're big egg people). This recipe puts an Italian twist on Turkish eggs (*çilbir*), swapping the traditional yoghurt base for garlicky whipped ricotta, and the smoky pul biber butter for a punchy tomato and chilli version. The result is *incredibly* delicious and, served with crusty bread, it makes for a simple but satisfying dinner (or brunch!).

*If **poaching eggs** feels like too much hassle for a quick midweek dinner, frying them works too.*

1 Bring a wide saucepan of water to a gentle simmer over a high heat. Line a large plate with kitchen paper.

2 While the water is coming to the boil, whisk the ricotta until smooth, then add the garlic and a pinch of salt and whisk again. Divide the ricotta mixture equally between two shallow bowls, using the back of a spoon to spread it out.

3 Melt the butter in a small saucepan over a high heat. Once melted, reduce the heat to medium and add the tomato purée and chilli flakes. Cook, whisking almost constantly, for 2–3 minutes, or until the mixture is fragrant and slightly darkened, then remove from the heat.

4 Reduce the heat of the saucepan of water to maintain a gentle simmer. Working one at a time, if necessary, crack each egg into a small bowl or ramekin and gently slide it into the simmering water. Poach for around 3 minutes, or until the whites are set but the yolks remain runny, then, using a slotted spoon, transfer the cooked egg to the plate lined with kitchen paper, leaving it to drain while you cook the remainder.

5 To serve, place two poached eggs into each bowl of whipped ricotta. Season with salt and pepper, then drizzle the tomato-chilli butter over the top. Garnish with basil leaves (if using) and serve immediately alongside crusty bread or toast.

Japanese Curry Ramen

Serves 4

1 litre vegetable stock
1 × 92g block of Japanese
   Golden Curry roux
2 tbsp mirin
150g frozen edamame beans
4 portions ramen noodles
   (dried, fresh or frozen –
   I prefer frozen for the texture,
   and they boil in just 1 minute)
300g silken tofu (or cooked
   protein of choice)
2 spring onions, thinly sliced
Pickled ginger and chilli oil,
   to serve

This is the ultimate lazy winter warmer. Japanese curry cubes are the shortcut here – they melt straight into the broth and bring instant depth of flavour. I usually go for S&B, which you can find in most large supermarkets, Asian stores or online. You whisk in a splash of mirin to round things out, then pile it all over bouncy ramen noodles with edamame, silken tofu (or your protein of choice) and whatever toppings you've got knocking about. It's simple, but hits every time.

1   Bring the stock to a simmer in a medium saucepan over a high heat. Add the curry roux and mirin and whisk to dissolve the block. Cover the pan, reduce the heat to low and leave the broth to simmer while you prep everything else.

2   In a separate pot, boil the edamame for a couple of minutes until tender, then scoop them out with a slotted spoon, drain and set aside.

3   Use the same water to cook the ramen noodles according to the package instructions, then drain them and divide them equally between four bowls.

4   Slice or spoon the silken tofu straight over the noodles – no need to warm it. Ladle the hot curry broth over everything, then top with the cooked edamame, and the spring onions, pickled ginger and a drizzle of chilli oil. Serve immediately.

Broccoli Caesar Pasta Salad

**Serves 4
with leftovers**

400g dried orzo
150g mayonnaise
4–6 anchovy fillets in oil,
  drained, to taste (I go for
  the full 6!)
1 garlic clove
4 heaped tbsp
  grated parmesan
1 tbsp lemon juice, or more
  to taste
1 tsp Dijon mustard, or more
  to taste
400g longstem broccoli, cut
  into bite-sized pieces

**For the anchovy crumb
(optional, but highly
recommended)**
2 tbsp extra-virgin olive oil
2 anchovy fillets
60g panko breadcrumbs

If you're afraid of anchovies, you might think this recipe isn't for you – but I urge you to try it anyway! Yes, they're in the dressing *and* in the crumb, but nothing about this pasta salad tastes fishy. When you cook anchovies down or blitz them into a creamy dressing, that briny fishiness mellows out completely. What you're left with is pure, savoury umami depth – the kind of flavour you'd struggle to get from anything else.

I've gone for a pasta salad here instead of the traditional leafy Caesar because if I'm going to have a salad for dinner, it needs to actually feel like dinner. The orzo gives it a bit of chew, the broccoli keeps things nice and fresh and the dressing pulls everything together. The anchovy crumb is optional but highly, highly recommended – it's salty, crispy and brings some much-needed crunch.

1 Boil the orzo in plenty of well-salted water according to the package instructions. Add the broccoli for the final 2 minutes of cooking, then drain both and rinse them under cold water.

2 While the orzo cooks, make the dressing. Add the mayonnaise, anchovies, garlic, parmesan, lemon juice and mustard to a small food processor with a pinch of salt and plenty of black pepper. Blitz until smooth and creamy.

3 If you're making the anchovy crumb, heat the olive oil in a small frying pan over a medium to medium-high heat. Add the anchovies and break them up with the back of a spoon – they should melt into the oil. I'll be honest, this won't smell great (very, very fishy), but don't worry – the fishiness will mellow out, leaving behind lots of savoury umami goodness. Stir in the panko breadcrumbs and cook, stirring frequently, for 3–4 minutes, or until golden and crisp. Set aside.

4 Transfer the drained orzo and broccoli to a large bowl, add the dressing and toss to coat. Taste and adjust the seasoning.

5 Divide the salad between your serving bowls (or as much as you think people want, with leftovers) and finish with a generous scattering of the anchovy crumb.

Satay-ish Chickpea & Spinach Curry

Serves 4

1 × 400g tin of chickpeas,
  drained and rinsed
2 × 400g tins of good-quality
  coconut milk (70% or more
  coconut extract)
100g smooth natural
  peanut butter
1 tbsp good-quality Thai red
  curry paste
1 tbsp mild curry powder
1 tbsp light soy sauce
1 tsp sugar
200ml boiling water
200g baby spinach
½ lime, juice

To serve

Cooked rice and/or
  warmed flatbreads
Roasted peanuts, finely
  chopped (optional)

This is the ultimate curry in a hurry, made with just a handful of storecupboard staples, in one pan and in just 15 minutes. It's got everything: warmth from the spices, richness from the peanut butter and coconut milk and freshness from a final hit of lime and spinach. It's comforting but not heavy, simple but packed with flavour – an easy fix for when you want a deeply satisfying dinner, fast.

*Good-quality **Thai curry pastes** are made with fresh, natural ingredients like Thai chillies, lemongrass, galangal, lime leaves and shrimp paste. Look for brands that use a high percentage of these and avoid those padded out with additives or preservatives. I highly recommend Thai Taste (which is vegan) and Mae Ploy.*

1 Place the chickpeas, coconut milk, peanut butter, curry paste, curry powder, soy sauce and sugar in a medium saucepan and set it over a high heat.

2 Stir in the boiling water and bring the liquid to a simmer, stirring frequently to prevent the curry sauce sticking. Reduce the heat to medium–high and cook, again stirring frequently, for 5 minutes.

3 Add the baby spinach and lime juice, stirring until the spinach has wilted, then season with salt and pepper.

4 Serve the curry in bowls with rice and/or flatbreads, and if you want some crunch, scatter over a few roasted peanuts.

30 Minutes

I think 30 minutes feels like the perfect sweet spot. It's enough time to coax out deeper flavours and create more exciting meals, but short enough to still feel doable after a busy day.

Some of my favourite recipes live in this chapter. The Crispy Prawn Crumpets put a fun twist on the classic, with cornflakes for crunch and crumpets for a satisfyingly chewy base. Then there's my Sichuan Steak Frîtes – easily one of the most delicious recipes I've ever developed. Numbing Sichuan peppercorns meet a golden-crusted steak, finished with a sauce built with Shaoxing wine and warm aromatics. And finally, my Red & Green Dinner Party Salmon: a bold, two-tone fish dish slathered in smoky chipotle on one side and a zingy, herby green marinade on the other.

None of the dishes in this chapter are complicated, but they show how much you can accomplish in half an hour when you use time and technique to your advantage. High-temperature roasting gives you caramelisation and crisp edges. Steaming ingredients with aromatics helps build deep flavour. And spices, whether bloomed in hot oil or dry-toasted, bring extra depth. These dishes are layered and satisfying.

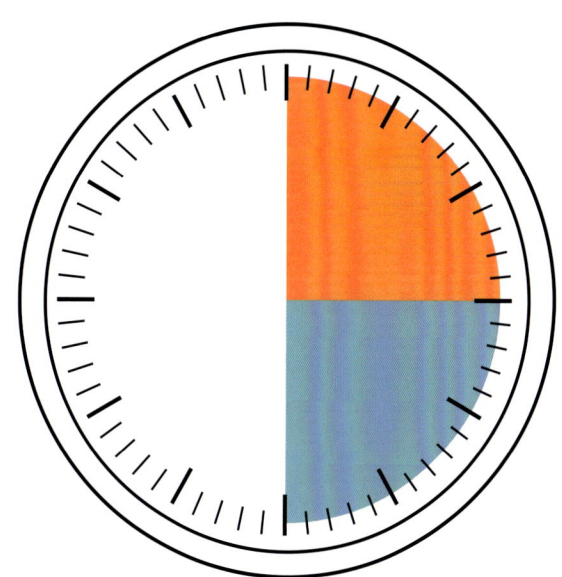

In this chapter

'Nduja Vodka Pasta

Serves 4

2 tbsp extra-virgin olive oil
2 banana shallots (echalions),
  very finely chopped
80g 'nduja
4 garlic cloves, finely grated
  or minced
120g double-concentrate
  tomato purée
75ml vodka
300ml double cream
1 tsp sugar (optional)
400g dried pasta of choice
50g parmigiano reggiano,
  grated, plus more to serve
1 handful of fresh basil leaves,
  to garnish

This spicy, saucy vodka pasta is perfect for a cosy night in. The addition of 'nduja brings a salty, funky twist to the classic, but if you leave it out, you're still in for a treat. Simply add an extra splash of olive oil – or better yet, a knob of butter – when softening the shallots and up the tomato purée to 200g.

Fun fact for the food nerds: the vodka isn't there just for the sake of it. It helps emulsify the sauce for that smooth, glossy finish, while also adding a richer, deeper flavour.

1 Bring a large pot of salted water to the boil over a high heat.

2 Meanwhile, heat the olive oil in a large sauté pan over a medium heat. Add the shallots, then reduce the heat to medium–low. Cook, stirring occasionally, for 5 minutes, or until softened.

3 Add the 'nduja, breaking it up with a wooden spoon. As it heats, it will begin to melt. Cook, stirring frequently, for 1 minute, then add the garlic and cook, again stirring frequently, for another 1 minute.

4 Turn the heat up to medium, then add the tomato purée and cook, again stirring frequently, until the purée begins to darken and caramelise (around 5 minutes). Add the vodka and stir well, scraping any browned bits from the bottom of the pan. Cook for 3 minutes, giving it all an occasional stir. Add the double cream and sugar (if using) and stir until well combined, then remove from the heat.

5 Add the pasta to the boiling salted water and cook according to the package instructions until al dente. Drain, reserving around 200ml of the cooking water.

6 Return the sauce to the hob over a medium heat. Add the pasta, parmigiano reggiano and a ladleful of the pasta cooking water. Cook, stirring constantly, until the pasta is well coated and glossy, loosening with a little more of the pasta water, if needed.

7 Divide the pasta between your serving bowls, garnish with the fresh basil and an extra sprinkle of parmigiano reggiano, then serve.

Aromatic Ginger & Spring Onion Steamed Cod

Serves 2

125g white jasmine rice or
   250g packet of microwavable
   sushi rice
2 cod fillets, or any flaky white
   fish (preferably with the skin)
½ tbsp Shaoxing wine
30g fresh ginger, peeled and
   cut into 5mm-ish slices,
   or julienned
1 × 7cm cinnamon stick
½ star anise
1 tbsp dark soy sauce
4 tbsp just-boiled water,
   plus more if you don't have
   a steamer
2 tsp sugar
1 spring onion, thinly sliced
1 small handful of fresh
   coriander, leaves and tender
   stems roughly chopped
2 tbsp vegetable oil (or any
   neutral oil)

This is my streamlined take on Cantonese steamed fish. The traditional version calls for a whole fish, carefully julienned aromatics, soy and sizzling-hot oil – it's brilliant, but a little labour-intensive. Here, I've adapted it for weeknight cooking. Instead of a whole fish, I use fillets, and the ginger is sliced (or julienned if you feel like being a bit fancy), and laid directly over the fish so that it softens as it steams. I also add cinnamon and star anise to the base of the dish, which isn't traditional, but I like the warmth they bring.

1   If you're cooking the rice from scratch, rinse it under cold water using a sieve or colander, then drain it well and tip it into a pot. Add 180ml of cold water and bring it to a simmer over a medium–high heat. Once simmering, cover the pot with a tight-fitting lid, turn the heat down to low and cook the rice for 12 minutes, until the grains are tender. Take the pot off the heat and let the rice sit, covered, for 3 minutes, then fluff it up with a fork. If you're using microwave packet rice, which I recommend here, heat it up just before serving.

2   If you have a steamer, skip to the next step. If not, place a heatproof rack or upturned bowl in a large, lidded saucepan and pour in enough boiling water to come three-quarters of the way up the rack or bowl. Cover and set over a high heat.

3   Pat the fish fillets dry and place them in a shallow, heatproof dish that fits inside your steamer. Drizzle over the Shaoxing wine and gently turn the fillets to coat. Scatter the ginger slices over the fish, then add the cinnamon stick and star anise to the base of the dish. Transfer the dish to the steamer, then cover it and lower the heat to medium. Steam for 8–10 minutes, or until the cod flakes easily.

4   To make a sauce, in a small bowl, stir together the soy sauce, sugar and the 4 tablespoons of boiling water until the sugar dissolves.

5   Once the fish is cooked, carefully tip out any juices that have pooled in the dish, then push the ginger slices to the base of the dish, alongside the star anise and cinnamon – they'll flavour the sauce. Pour the sauce over the fish, then scatter the spring onion and coriander directly on top.

6   Heat the oil in a saucepan until it shimmers, then pour it over the spring onion and coriander to sizzle. Serve immediately with the rice.

Red & Green Dinner Party Salmon

Serves 6

1.2kg skin-on salmon side
   (or 2 × 600g fillets)
Lime wedges, to serve

For the green side

2 large garlic cloves, peeled
15g fresh flat-leaf parsley
2 tbsp vegetable oil (or
   any neutral oil), plus more
   for greasing
¼ tsp ground cumin

For the red side

2 large garlic cloves, peeled
1 vine tomato, cored
   and deseeded
1 tsp chipotle chilli powder
2 tbsp vegetable oil (or any
   neutral oil)
1 tbsp freshly squeezed
   orange juice
¼ tsp ground cumin
¼ tsp ground cloves

To serve taco-style (optional)

4 warmed tortillas
400g refried beans, warmed
   (homemade or from a can)
Your favourite salsa
   (homemade or shop-bought)

This dish is my take on Contramar's famous red and green snapper, one of the best things I ate in Mexico City. I've swapped in salmon for easier sourcing but the real star – the punchy two-tone marinade – remains. The red side is smoky and rich while the green side is fresh and herby. This is the kind of dish that looks impressive but is easy to throw together. I love serving it as they do at Contramar – with warm corn tortillas, refried beans and salsas for a DIY taco spread – but it's just as good with rice, roasted veg and/or a crisp salad.

*The **spice amounts** in this recipe are very small but please don't be tempted to leave them out – they make a big difference!*

1   Heat your oven grill to 250°C. Line a large baking tray with foil and lightly grease it with oil. Score the salmon in a crosshatch pattern and place it on the prepared tray.

2   To make the green side, pound the garlic to a paste in a pestle and mortar, then add the parsley and bash again to a rough paste. (If you don't have a pestle and mortar, you can use a mini blender or food processor instead.) Mix in the oil and cumin and season with salt and pepper (the result should be well seasoned).

3   Spread this mixture down the length of one half of the salmon, making sure to work it into all the crosshatch grooves.

4   Wipe out the mortar, and move on to the red side. Pound the garlic to a paste, then add the tomato and chipotle chilli powder and bash to a rough paste. Mix in the oil, orange juice, cumin and cloves and season with salt and pepper (again, it should be well seasoned). Spread this over the other half of the salmon.

5   Grill the salmon for 12–15 minutes, or until just opaque and easily flaked with a fork. The exact time will depend on its thickness. Carefully transfer the salmon to a platter and serve it with lime wedges for squeezing over.

6   If you want to serve this taco-style, bring the salmon to the table with the warmed tortillas, refried beans and your favourite salsa and let everyone dig in to construct their own.

Crispy Coconut Sea Bass with Avocado & Mango Salsa

Serves 4

4 skin-on sea bass fillets
50g plain flour
1 tsp fine sea salt
1 tsp garlic granules or powder
1 tsp onion granules or powder
2 medium eggs
50g panko breadcrumbs
35g unsweetened
   desiccated coconut
Vegetable oil (or any neutral
   oil), for shallow-frying

**For the avocado
& mango salsa**

1 avocado, stoned, peeled and
   cut into small cubes
100g mango chunks, cut into
   small cubes
¼ red onion, very
   finely chopped
1 handful of fresh coriander,
   leaves and tender stems
   finely chopped
1 red chilli, minced (optional;
   deseed for less heat)
1 tbsp fresh lime juice, or more
   to taste

Fried fish is delicious, but I don't always want the heaviness that comes with it. This is my answer to that – sea bass coated in coconut and panko, shallow-fried until perfectly golden. The coconut adds great flavour, while the panko keeps the coating light and crisp. Paired with a fresh avocado and mango salsa, it's the perfect balance of crunchiness, sweetness and acidity.

1 First, make the salsa. Combine the avocado, mango, red onion, coriander, chilli (if using) and lime in a bowl. Season with salt and pepper, and mix gently. Taste and adjust the lime if needed. Refrigerate until you're ready to serve.

2 Pat the sea bass fillets dry with kitchen paper.

3 In a shallow dish, combine the flour, salt, and garlic and onion granules or powder. In another dish, beat the eggs with a good pinch of salt and pepper. In a third dish, combine the panko breadcrumbs and desiccated coconut.

4 Dredge each fillet in the seasoned flour, shaking off any excess; then into the egg, turning to coat and letting the excess drip off; then in the panko and coconut mixture, pressing firmly so it adheres evenly with no bare spots.

5 Once all the fillets are coated, heat 1–2cm of oil in a large frying pan over a medium or medium–high heat. Once hot, place the fillets in the pan and fry for 2 minutes, or until the underside is golden and crisp. Flip and cook for another 2 minutes, or until golden and crisp all over.

6 Transfer the fish to a wire rack or to a plate lined with kitchen paper to drain, then serve with the avocado and mango salsa spooned over the top.

Summer Tomato & Strawberry Panzanella

Serves 2-3

300g mixed ripe tomatoes,
    cut into bite-sized pieces
½ tsp fine sea salt
150g day-old sourdough
    or ciabatta, cut into
    2–3cm cubes
4 tbsp extra-virgin olive oil
2 tbsp white wine vinegar
½ banana shallot (echalion),
    finely chopped
250g strawberries, hulled, and
    halved if small or quartered
    if large
10g fresh basil leaves, torn

This dish is a celebration of summer's finest produce. In its purest form, panzanella is a humble Tuscan salad, typically made with tomatoes, onions and cucumber, and designed to breathe new life into stale bread. Here, I've given it an extra summery twist by pairing juicy tomatoes with sweet strawberries, which are a surprising match made in heaven. It's bright and fresh, but still hearty enough to eat as a lunch or light dinner.

Hold out for peak summer to make this – its beauty hinges entirely on the ripeness of the tomatoes and strawberries. It doesn't shine quite as bright (no pun intended) when made out of season.

1   Heat your oven to 180°C/160°C fan.

2   Place the tomatoes in a sieve, sprinkle with the ½ teaspoon of salt and leave to drain for 15 minutes – this helps draw out excess moisture, which makes the tomatoes extra flavourful.

3   Meanwhile, toss the sourdough chunks with 1 tablespoon of the olive oil, season with salt and pepper and spread the chunks over a baking tray in a single layer. Bake the chunks for 15 minutes, or until crisp and firm but not browned.

4   In a large bowl, whisk together the remaining olive oil with the white wine vinegar and shallot. Season with salt and pepper to taste.

5   Add the toasted sourdough and drained tomatoes, along with the strawberries and half of the basil leaves to the bowl. Gently toss everything together to combine, then taste and adjust the seasoning, if needed.

6   Transfer the panzanella to a big plate, scatter over the remaining basil leaves, and serve.

Sichuan Steak Frîtes

Serves 2

200g frozen French fries
1 tsp black peppercorns
1 tsp Sichuan peppercorns
2 tbsp vegetable oil (or any
    neutral oil)
2 beef fillet steaks
    (around 170g each), at
    room temperature
2 tbsp butter
1 garlic clove, smashed
1 star anise
1 × 7cm cinnamon stick
1 banana shallot (echalion),
    finely chopped
1 tbsp Shaoxing wine
100ml good-quality rich
    beef stock
100ml double cream
Green salad, to serve

This is *steak frîtes* with a twist – a Chinese-inspired twist, to be precise. It might sound a little rogue, but it's genuinely one of the most delicious recipes I've ever developed. The steak is crusted on one side only with a mixture of black and Sichuan peppercorns, giving you the best of both worlds: a well-toasted peppercorn crust and beautifully seared beef.

Instead of the usual brandy, the sauce is built with Shaoxing wine and a handful of aromatics that bring warmth, complexity and balance. It's rich, deeply flavourful and just so good. Served with air-fried frozen French fries (who's making chips from scratch after work?), it's the ultimate treat-yourself dinner – and perfect for a date night.

1   Heat your air fryer to 200°C. Add the fries to the basket and cook for 10-15 minutes, depending on the size and power output of the air fryer, or until light golden and crisp. Alternatively, you can oven bake them according to the package instructions.

2   Crush the black peppercorns in a pestle and mortar until coarsely ground, then add the Sichuan peppercorns and crush again – you want a mixture of coarse and fine peppercorns. Tip the pepper mixture on to a plate.

3   Heat the oil in a medium stainless steel or cast-iron frying pan over a medium–high heat until shimmering.

4   Meanwhile, pat the steaks dry and season both sides with salt. Press one side of each steak into the pepper mixture to form a crust. Don't worry if some of the peppercorns are left behind – we'll use them in the sauce.

5   Place the steaks in the hot pan, pepper-side down, and sear for around 3 minutes, or until the peppercorns are well toasted.

6   Carefully flip the steaks, trying to keep that crust intact, then add the butter, garlic, star anise and cinnamon stick and cook for another 2-3 minutes, basting the steaks as you go.

continued overleaf...

7   Transfer the steaks to a plate to rest, loosely covered with foil. This should give you a medium-rare finish, although it'll depend on thickness. If your steaks are still too rare, pop them into a 190°C/170°C fan oven for a few minutes.

8   Leave the butter and the steak drippings in the pan, but remove the garlic, star anise and cinnamon. Lower the heat to medium and add the shallot and any remaining peppercorns from the plate, plus a good pinch of salt. Cook, stirring occasionally, for 3–5 minutes, or until the shallots are softened but not browned.

9   Pour in the Shaoxing wine and deglaze the pan, scraping up any caramelised bits. Let the wine bubble away and fully reduce, then add the beef stock and double cream and stir to combine. Simmer the sauce until it thickens enough to coat the back of a spoon. Taste and season with salt, if needed.

10 Return the steaks to the pan and spoon the sauce over the top of them to warm them through. Serve straight away with your hot fries and a zingy green salad.

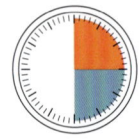

Crispy Chicken Thighs with Pistachio Vinaigrette & Lemony Potatoes

Serves 4

6 skin-on, bone-in
  chicken thighs
60g roasted pistachio kernels
  (ideally unsalted, but salted
  works too)
1 garlic clove, peeled
10g fresh basil or
  flat-leaf parsley
4 tbsp extra-virgin olive oil
1 tbsp red wine vinegar
1 tbsp runny honey

For the potatoes

750g small new potatoes
  (halved if larger)
3-4 tbsp extra-virgin olive oil
½-1 lemon, juice

The key to making the crispiest, most delicious chicken thighs is starting them skin-side down in a cold, dry pan. As the heat gradually builds, the fat slowly renders, which not only gives you that deep golden brown skin, but also allows the chicken to cook gently in its own juices. Once the chicken's perfectly crispy, it gets a generous spoonful of pistachio vinaigrette – zingy, nutty, a little sweet and full of texture. It cuts through the richness and brings everything to life. Serve it with the lemony potatoes, and steamed greens, if you like.

1   Start the potatoes. Place them in a large pot and cover with cold water. Season very generously with salt (potatoes really need it!). Cover the pot and bring the water to the boil. Then, reduce the heat and simmer for 10–15 minutes, or until the potatoes are tender.

2   While the potatoes cook, debone the chicken thighs (it's easier than you think!): place one of the thighs skin-side down on a chopping board. Use a small, sharp knife to cut along the bone to expose it, then slide the knife underneath and cut it out, keeping close to the bone to avoid losing meat. Repeat with the rest of the thighs. Pat the thighs dry and season them on both sides with salt.

3   Arrange the thighs in a single layer skin-side down in a cold, large non-stick or cast-iron pan. Set the pan over a medium heat, then cook the chicken, undisturbed, for 12–15 minutes, or until the skin is deeply golden and releases easily from the pan. Flip the thighs and cook them for another 3–5 minutes, or until cooked through. The exact cooking time will depend on their size and thickness.

4   While the chicken cooks, drain the potatoes and tip them into a large mixing bowl. Add the olive oil and lemon juice to taste, season with salt and pepper and toss to coat. Set aside to cool slightly.

5   In a food processor, pulse the pistachios and garlic until coarsely chopped. Add the basil or parsley, olive oil, vinegar and honey, and blitz to a chunky, pesto-like sauce (alternatively, you can do this in a pestle and mortar). Taste, and season with salt and pepper.

6   To serve, spoon the pistachio vinaigrette over the crispy chicken and serve with the lemony potatoes.

One-Pan Thai Curry Salmon with Coconut Rice

Serves 6

3 tbsp vegetable oil (or any neutral oil)
1 tbsp good-quality Thai red curry paste (see note, page 60)
6 salmon fillets (skin on or off)
350g jasmine rice
250ml coconut cream
4 makrut lime leaves, finely chopped (or the zest of 2 limes)
1 tsp fine sea salt
1 small handful of fresh coriander, chopped, to garnish

For the sauce
50g sweet chilli sauce
1 lime, juice

This is one of those recipes that does a lot with very little. You build layers of flavour into the rice using coconut cream and lime leaves, then nestle in salmon that's been marinated in good-quality Thai red curry paste. The fish finishes under the grill, taking on a little char while the rice continues to steam underneath. It's rich, fragrant and deeply satisfying – and it all happens in one pan, without any complicated steps. Great for a weeknight, but also impressive enough for guests.

It's worth going the extra mile (perhaps literally) to source makrut lime leaves. They have a unique citrusy, slightly floral brightness that pairs beautifully with the richness of the coconut, taking the rice from a 10/10 to a 12/10. But if you can't find them, don't worry – lime zest delivers plenty of the freshness you need.

1   Heat your oven grill to high. In a large bowl, combine the oil and Thai curry paste with a generous pinch of salt and pepper. Add the salmon fillets and toss to coat, then set them aside to marinate while you prepare the rice.

2   Wash the rice in cold water until the water runs clear. Drain it well and tip it into a wide ovenproof sauté pan or shallow casserole dish.

3   Add the coconut cream, lime leaves or lime zest, teaspoon of salt and 300ml of cold water and stir to combine. Bring the liquid to a simmer over a medium–high heat, then cover, reduce the heat to low and cook for 10 minutes.

4   Uncover the pan and arrange the seasoned salmon fillets in a single layer over the rice (skin down if they have the skin). Transfer the pan to the grill for 6–10 minutes, or until the salmon is lightly charred on top and just cooked through. The exact timing will depend on the thickness of your fillets.

5   While the salmon and rice are under the grill, stir together the sweet chilli sauce and lime juice. Drizzle this over the salmon and rice just before serving, then garnish with the coriander.

Tomato & Red Pepper Pesto Pasta

Serves 4

60g blanched or
  flaked almonds
Boiling water
400g linguine (or your
  preferred dried pasta)
2 garlic cloves, peeled
20g fresh basil leaves, plus
  more to serve
100g parmigiano reggiano,
  grated, plus more to serve
250g vine tomatoes,
  deseeded and quartered
1 roasted red pepper
  from a jar (about 150g),
  roughly chopped
60ml extra-virgin olive oil

When you say pesto, most people think of pesto alla Genovese – the bright green basil pesto we all know and love. But Italy has lots of regional pestos, each with its own twist. One of my favourites is pesto alla Trapanese, a Sicilian pesto made with almonds, tomatoes, garlic and basil. This is my take on it, with the addition of roasted red peppers for extra depth and sweetness. It's vibrant, rich and comes together in minutes – perfect for a quick weeknight dinner.

1 In a large pot over a medium heat, toast the almonds, stirring frequently, until golden and browned in places, then transfer them to a food processor and leave them to cool slightly.

2 Pour boiling water into the same pot and season very, very generously with salt. Boil the pasta according to the package instructions, reserving a cupful of pasta water before draining.

3 Meanwhile, in a food processor, blitz the toasted almonds and garlic until roughly chopped. Add the basil, parmigiano reggiano, tomatoes, roasted red pepper and olive oil, then blitz to a rough paste. Season with salt and pepper, to taste. Alternatively, you can do this in a large pestle and mortar.

4 Return the drained pasta to the pot and toss it with the pesto, loosening with a splash of the reserved pasta water, as needed, until glossy and well-coated. Taste and adjust the seasoning, if necessary.

5 Serve topped with extra parmigiano reggiano and a few torn basil leaves.

Mouthwatering Sichuan Chicken

Serves 4

650g boneless, skinless
chicken thigh fillets
(around 6)
25g fresh ginger, peeled and
thinly sliced
4 spring onions,
halved horizontally
1 tbsp fine sea salt (this sounds
like a lot but don't worry,
the chicken won't absorb
much of it)

For the sauce

2 tsp Sichuan peppercorns
(halve to reduce the
numbing heat)
2 large garlic cloves, finely
grated or minced
2 tsp chilli flakes (halve to
make a milder sauce)
3 tbsp vegetable oil (or
any neutral oil)
2 tbsp light soy sauce
1 tbsp toasted sesame oil
1 tbsp toasted sesame seeds
1 tbsp rice vinegar
1 tbsp sugar
2 spring onions, thinly sliced
(reserve some greens
for garnish)

To serve
250g white jasmine rice

If there's one dish that perfectly encapsulates my love for Sichuan flavours, it's this one. It's a glorious mashup of two beloved staples: the famously spicy and numbing *kou shui ji* and the nutty, sesame-forward *bangbang ji*.

Here, tender chicken thighs are gently poached with ginger and spring onions until perfectly juicy, then topped with a vibrant sauce, packed with garlic, chilli, sesame and Sichuan peppercorns, which bring a numbing, tingling heat. Bold yet beautifully balanced, it's delicious served warm or chilled, preferably with hot rice.

If you'd prefer something a bit milder (true to its Sichuan inspiration, this dish brings plenty of spice and heat), halve the amounts of Sichuan peppercorns and chilli flakes.

1   Place the chicken thigh fillets, ginger, halved spring onions and salt in a large saucepan and cover with 1.5 litres of cold water. Place the pan over a medium–high heat and bring the water to a gentle simmer.

2   Cover the pan, reduce the heat to low and poach the thighs for 10–12 minutes, or until cooked through. The chicken should feel firm but springy when gently pressed.

3   To prepare the rice to serve, rinse it under cold water using a sieve or colander, then drain it well and tip it into a pot. Add 360ml of cold water and bring the water to a simmer over a medium–high heat. Once simmering, cover the pot with a tight-fitting lid, turn the heat down to low and cook the rice for 12 minutes, until the water has been absorbed and the grains are tender. Take the pot off the heat and let the rice sit, covered, for 3 minutes, then fluff it up with a fork.

4   While the rice cooks, place the Sichuan peppercorns in a pestle and mortar and grind them to a coarse powder. Add the garlic and chilli flakes and pound them to a rough paste.

5 Heat the vegetable oil in a small saucepan over a medium heat until shimmering, then pour it on to the garlic and peppercorn paste and stir well to combine.

6 Add the light soy sauce, sesame oil, sesame seeds, rice vinegar and sugar and chopped spring onions (except for the reserved greens). Mix everything to combine and set aside. This is your sauce base.

7 If you're intending to serve the dish cold, transfer the poached chicken (reserving the cooking liquid) to a bowl of iced water and leave it to cool for 5–10 minutes. If you're serving the dish warm, transfer the chicken (still reserving the liquid) to a chopping board and rest it for 5–10 minutes.

8 Measure out 120ml of the reserved chicken poaching liquid and stir this into the sauce base to finish the sauce.

9 Divide your fluffy, steamed rice between four shallow serving bowls. Slice the chicken (drained and patted dry, if you've had it in the ice bath) and arrange it equally on top of the rice. Pour the sauce over the top and serve garnished with the reserved slivers of spring-onion greens.

Gochujang Butter Loco Moco

Serves 4

250g white jasmine rice
  or 500g packet of
  microwavable sushi rice
Vegetable oil (or any
  neutral oil)
4 quarter pounder
  beef burgers
2 tbsp unsalted butter
1 large onion, thinly sliced
500ml beef stock
2 tbsp gochujang
1 tbsp light soy sauce
1 tbsp sugar
1 tbsp cornflour, mixed with
  2 tbsp water
4 large eggs

Loco Moco is the perfect comfort dish – a juicy homemade burger smothered in a rich gravy, served over rice and topped with a fried egg. This version takes a few shortcuts while dialling up the flavour. Instead of making the patties from scratch, I use shop-bought burgers, which makes this even more of a low-effort, high-reward meal. The real star is the gochujang butter gravy – rich, deep, savoury and just a little bit spicy. It's simple, bold and exactly the kind of thing you want to eat when only proper comfort food will do.

1 If you're cooking the rice from scratch, rinse it under cold water using a sieve or colander, then drain it well and tip it into a pot. Add 360ml of cold water and bring it to a simmer over a medium–high heat. Once simmering, cover the pot with a tight-fitting lid, turn the heat down to low and cook the rice for 12 minutes, until the grains are tender. Take the pot off the heat and let the rice sit, covered, for 3 minutes, then fluff it up with a fork. If you're using microwave packet rice, which I recommend here, heat it up just before serving.

2 Meanwhile, heat a teaspoon or two of oil in a large, deep non-stick frying pan over a high heat. Add the burgers and sear them until they are deeply browned on both sides (around 2 minutes per side). Transfer the burgers to a plate.

3 Pour out any excess oil in the pan, leaving any browned bits behind. Reduce the heat to medium and add the butter. Once melted, add the onion and cook, stirring occasionally, until softened and beginning to caramelise (around 10 minutes). Add the beef stock, gochujang, soy sauce and sugar and stir to combine. Bring the liquid to a simmer, then cover the pan and cook for 10 minutes.

4 Stir in the cornflour slurry and let the gravy thicken (about 1–2 minutes), then return the burgers to the pan, spooning some sauce over them. Cover the pot, and simmer the gravy for 2–3 minutes, or until the burgers are heated through.

5 Meanwhile, heat a little oil in a separate frying pan over a medium heat. Crack in the eggs and fry them for around 3 minutes, until the whites are set but the yolks remain runny.

6 Serve the burgers over the steamed rice. Top with plenty of the gochujang butter gravy and finish each portion with a fried egg.

Teriyaki Pork Miso Ramen

Serves 2

For the broth

1 litre dashi
30g white miso paste
30g good-quality tahini
2 tbsp dark soy sauce
10g fresh ginger, peeled and
   finely grated or minced
2 large garlic cloves, finely
   grated or minced

For the pork

Vegetable oil (or any
   neutral oil)
250g pork mince
2 tbsp dark soy sauce
2 tbsp mirin
1 tbsp sugar

For the ramen

2 portions of ramen noodles
   (dried, fresh or frozen –
   I prefer frozen for the texture,
   and they boil in just 1 minute)
2 pak choi, halved lengthways
2 spring onions, thinly sliced
Toppings of choice, such
   as chilli oil, sesame seeds,
   shichimi togarashi, soft-
   boiled egg and/or seaweed

This ramen is so incredibly flavourful, which is surprising given that the broth comes together in just 5 minutes. The secret weapon is instant dashi, which packs a massive umami-rich punch that makes any broth taste like it's been simmering for hours. I've used pork here, but you could easily swap in chicken, lamb or beef; or for a vegan version, try plant-based mince or crumbled extra-firm tofu. Whatever protein you use, just toss it in the three-ingredient teriyaki sauce and you're golden. Finish with your favourite toppings.

*Not all **tahini** is created equal. Good tahini is smooth, pourable and well balanced. Bad tahini is thick, clumpy, gritty and, worst of all, unbearably bitter. Where possible, go for a Middle Eastern brand over a supermarket own label. Some of my favourite tahini brands are Baracke, Al Nakhil, Al Taj and Belazu.*

1 Pour the dashi into a saucepan and bring it to a simmer over a medium–high heat.

2 In a heatproof bowl, whisk together the miso paste, tahini, soy sauce, ginger and garlic. Add a ladleful or two of the hot dashi, whisk until smooth, then pour it all back into the pot, whisking to combine. Taste and season with salt if needed, depending on the saltiness of your dashi. Set aside. It may split slightly as it cools – that's normal.

3 For the pork, heat a splash of oil in a frying pan or wok over a high heat. Add the mince and cook, breaking it up with a spoon, until there's no pink left. Add the soy sauce, mirin and sugar and cook for 2 minutes, or until thickened and glossy. Set aside.

4 To make the ramen, boil the noodles in salted water according to the package instructions, adding the pak choi for the final 1 minute. Drain, and divide the noodles and pak choi between two serving bowls.

5 Reheat the broth and ladle it over the noodles and pak choi (depending on how brothy you like your ramen, you may have broth left over – it will freeze beautifully for another time). Top with the teriyaki pork, spring onions and any extra toppings you like, then serve immediately.

Steamed Pork & Prawn Cabbage Rolls

Serves 4

8 large outer savoy
  cabbage leaves (or
  use Chinese leaves)
200g pork mince (20% fat
  – any less and the filling will
  be dry, not juicy)
200g deveined, peeled raw
  king prawns, finely chopped
2 spring onions, very
  thinly sliced
10g fresh ginger, finely grated
  or minced
2 tbsp toasted sesame oil
1 tbsp Shaoxing wine
1 tbsp light soy sauce
1 tbsp oyster sauce
Sweet chilli sauce, to
  serve (optional)

**For the dipping
sauce (optional)**
2 tbsp light soy sauce
1 tbsp rice vinegar
1 tsp sugar
1 tsp Chinese chilli oil

Dumplings are one of my favourite things to eat, but I don't always have the time (or patience) to wrap and pleat them. These cabbage rolls deliver the same satisfaction, with less effort and a lighter feel. The cabbage locks in moisture, keeping the filling plump and juicy, and adds a delicate sweetness of its own. I like to serve them straight from the steamer with a simple but punchy dipping sauce.

1 Blanch the cabbage leaves in generously salted boiling water for 1–2 minutes, or until they are just wilted. Drain the leaves, rinse them under cold water, then spread them out on to a clean tea towel to dry while you make the filling.

2 In a medium bowl, combine the pork mince, prawns, spring onions, ginger, sesame oil, Shaoxing wine, soy sauce and oyster sauce. Mix well until the mixture turns sticky and paste-like.

3 Place an eighth of the filling in the centre of each cabbage leaf. Roll each leaf tightly into a cylinder, tucking in the sides as you go.

4 Arrange the rolls, seam-side down, on a heatproof plate and place them in a steamer lined with baking paper. Steam for 8–10 minutes, or until the filling is cooked through. If you don't have a steamer, place the heatproof plate on a small, inverted bowl inside a large, lidded pan. Add a few centimetres of boiling water, cover, and steam as usual.

5 Meanwhile, if you're serving with the dipping sauce, combine all the sauce ingredients in a bowl and set aside.

6 When the rolls are ready, serve them immediately with the optional dipping sauce or sweet chilli sauce.

Crispy Prawn Crumpets

Makes 6

320g deveined, peeled raw
   king prawns
10g fresh ginger, peeled and
   finely grated or minced
1 egg white
½ tbsp light soy sauce
1 tsp toasted sesame oil
1 tsp Shaoxing wine (optional)
1 tbsp cornflour
½ tsp sugar
2 spring onions, very
   thinly sliced
6 crumpets
50g cornflakes, crushed
Vegetable oil (or any
   neutral oil)
Sweet chilli sauce or sriracha
   mayo, to serve

One of my friends, chef Angelica Udenweze, once made the best prawn toast I'd ever had. She swapped the sesame seeds for cornflakes, making it irresistibly crispy – it was absolute perfection. This recipe takes inspiration from hers, but instead of white bread, I'm using crumpets, which, in my opinion, have one of the best bread textures of all time. They crisp up beautifully on the outside, while their soft, spongy interior soaks up all the prawn juices, making every bite extra juicy and flavourful.

1 Drain any excess moisture from the prawns. Coarsely chop half of them and transfer these to a medium mixing bowl.

2 In a food processor, blend the remaining prawns with the ginger, egg white, soy sauce, sesame oil, Shaoxing wine (if using), cornflour and sugar until smooth. Add this mixture and the spring onions to the bowl with the coarsely chopped prawns and mix to combine.

3 Spread the prawn mixture evenly over the six crumpets, making sure each one is fully covered in an even layer.

4 Place the crushed cornflakes in a bowl. Gently press each crumpet into the cornflakes, prawn-side down, letting any excess fall away. Warm your oven to 150°C/130°C fan.

5 Pour 3–4cm of oil into a large, deep-sided sauté pan or frying pan and heat it to 180°C. If you don't have a thermometer, dip the handle of a wooden spoon into the oil – the oil will bubble rapidly around the handle when it's ready for frying. Carefully lower 2 or 3 crumpets into the oil (depending on the size of your pan – don't overcrowd it), prawn-side down, and fry for 2 minutes, or until the underside is golden brown. Flip and fry for a further 2 minutes, or until the other side is golden brown too.

6 Transfer the cooked crumpets to a plate lined with kitchen paper to drain, then keep them warm in the oven while frying the rest. Serve hot with sweet chilli sauce or sriracha mayo for dipping.

Steam-Fried Teriyaki Aubergine

Serves 2

125g white jasmine rice or
250g packet of microwavable
sushi rice
Boiling water, if you don't have
a steamer
2 small aubergines (long, slim
ones are best)
2 tbsp dark soy sauce
2 tbsp mirin
2 tsp sugar
2 tbsp vegetable oil
1 spring onion, thinly sliced
Toasted sesame seeds,
to garnish

I used to be the *biggest* aubergine hater. That changed when a friend made me some roasted aubergines with curried yoghurt and pomegranate (an Ottolenghi favourite). Until then, I'd always found aubergines to be tough, rubbery and unpleasantly chewy. But these were soft and squidgy – the good kind – and deeply flavourful. Dramatic as this may sound, that moment marked the start of my (so far) decade-long love affair with aubergines. Here, the aubergines are steamed until completely tender, then flattened and pan-seared until golden and caramelised.

1   If you're cooking the rice from scratch, rinse it under cold water using a sieve or colander, then drain it well and tip it into a pot. Add 180ml of water and bring to a simmer over a medium–high heat. Cover the pot with a tight-fitting lid, turn the heat down to low and cook the rice for 12 minutes, until tender. Let the rice sit, covered, off the heat, for 3 minutes, then fluff it up with a fork. If you're using microwave packet rice, which I recommend here, heat it up just before serving.

2   If you have a steamer, skip to the next step. If not, place a heatproof rack or upturned bowl in a large, lidded saucepan and pour in enough boiling water to come three-quarters of the way up the rack or bowl. Cover and set over a high heat.

3   Peel the aubergines and trim off the ends, then halve them crossways so you have four shorter pieces. Steam the aubergine pieces for 16–18 minutes, or until a knife slides through them with no resistance.

4   While the aubergines are steaming, mix the dark soy sauce, mirin, sugar and 2 tablespoons of water in a small bowl. This is your sauce.

5   Cool the aubergines for 5 minutes, then halve each piece lengthways – cutting almost all the way through but leaving a hinge. Open the pieces out like a book, then use a fork to gently flatten each one into a wide, cutlet-like shape.

6   Heat the oil in a large non-stick frying pan over a high heat. Add the 'cutlets' and brown them on both sides (about 1 minute per side). Pour the sauce into the pan and cook, shaking the pan occasionally, for 1–2 minutes, or until the sauce thickens to coat the aubergine. Serve the aubergine over hot rice, topped with the spring onion and a sprinkle of toasted sesame seeds.

Numbing Cumin Lamb Noodles

Serves 4–5

2 tbsp cumin seeds
2 tsp Sichuan peppercorns
2 tsp chilli flakes
100ml vegetable oil (or any neutral oil), plus more for frying the mince
2 tbsp oyster sauce
2 tbsp light soy sauce
2 tbsp Chinese black vinegar (or rice vinegar)
2 tbsp Shaoxing wine
2 tsp sugar
500g lamb mince (10% fat)
6 large garlic cloves, finely grated or minced
4 spring onions, thinly sliced, whites and greens separated
1 handful of fresh coriander, leaves and tender stems roughly chopped
400g dried noodles (or 4 portions of fresh hand-pulled noodles, if you can find some)

This dish pulls influence from northwestern China – Xi'an, to be precise – where cumin and chilli often come together in bold, savoury dishes. I was first introduced to this flavour profile at Xi'an Famous Foods in New York. This recipe is my take on their legendary spicy cumin lamb noodles. Their version uses thinly sliced lamb shoulder, a proprietary sauce made with 30 (!) different spices and chewy hand-pulled noodles – no wonder it's so good! Mine uses lamb mince, fewer spices and dried noodles, but it's still packed with flavour: spice-forward, deeply savoury and very satisfying.

You can swap the lamb for beef, pork or chicken mince. *For a meat-free version,* use plant-based mince, crumbled tofu or pulled oyster mushrooms.

1 Toast the cumin seeds and Sichuan peppercorns in a dry small saucepan over a medium heat until fragrant (around 1 minute).

2 Transfer the seeds and peppercorns to a mortar and pound them to a coarse mixture, then tip this back into the saucepan and add the chilli flakes and oil. Bring the oil to a gentle sizzle over a medium heat, then remove the pan from the heat and stir in the oyster sauce, soy sauce, black vinegar (or rice vinegar), Shaoxing wine, and sugar. Set aside – this is your sauce.

3 Heat a little oil in a large wok or sauté pan over a high heat. Add the lamb mince, breaking it up with a wooden spoon, and stir-fry until the water evaporates and the mince starts to brown (around 7 minutes).

4 Add the garlic and the white parts of the spring onions and stir-fry for 1 minute, then pour in the sauce and let it bubble for 1 minute. Remove the pan from the heat and stir through the coriander.

5 Boil the noodles in salted water according to the package instructions. Drain well, then divide them equally between your serving bowls and spoon over the lamb mixture. Top with the spring-onion greens and toss everything together just before eating.

Spicy Salmon Crispy Rice Bowls

Serves 2

2 tbsp Kewpie mayonnaise
(see note, page 189)
1–2 tbsp sriracha (depending
on how spicy you like it)
2 tsp toasted sesame oil
2 spring onions, thinly sliced
(reserve some of the greens
for garnish)
250g sushi-grade skinless
salmon fillet, cut into
1cm cubes
100g baby cucumber,
thinly sliced
1 tsp light soy sauce
1 tsp lime juice
½ tbsp vegetable oil (or any
neutral oil)
250g packet of microwavable
sushi rice (squeeze to
separate the grains)
100g mango chunks
Sprinkle of shichimi
togarashi (optional)

This bowl is all about contrast and balance – hot and cold, crispy and soft, fresh and rich, savoury and sweet. The salmon is tossed in a sesame-forward sriracha mayo, extra saucy so it can dress the rice too. Said rice is packed into a hot pan and toasted until golden and crispy. The cucumber is quick-pickled in soy and lime to bring brightness and zing, while the mango adds cool, juicy sweetness to round everything out. It's vibrant, textural and so satisfying.

*Swap in tuna for the salmon, if you prefer. And, **you can use tinned salmon or tuna**, if raw fish is an absolute no for you – although, in my opinion, the results won't be as delicious. If you do go down that route, opt for good-quality, oil-packed fish – the 'in water' or 'in brine' ones can be a little dry.*

1   In a medium bowl, mix the Kewpie mayo, sriracha and sesame oil. Add the spring onions (except for the reserved greens) to the bowl along with the salmon. Toss to coat, then refrigerate until you're ready to serve. The mixture should be quite saucy – it doubles as the 'dressing' for the crispy rice.

2   In a small bowl, toss the cucumber with the soy sauce and lime juice. Refrigerate while you make the rice.

3   Heat the vegetable oil in a large non-stick frying pan over a medium-high heat. Add the rice and press it into an even layer, like you would a rosti. Cook, undisturbed, for 5 minutes, or until the bottom is light golden brown and crisp. You can flip and cook the other side for 2–3 minutes if you like, but I prefer one side crisp and the other soft – it creates a delightful crispy-chewy texture.

4   To serve, build your bowls with crispy rice, spicy salmon, marinated cucumber, and mango. Finish with the reserved spring-onion greens and a sprinkle of shichimi togarashi, if using.

Kimchi Tofu Stew

Serves 4

600g firm tofu
200g drained kimchi (see
   note, page 34)
2 vine tomatoes (about 150g),
   cut into wedges
1 onion, thinly sliced
2 garlic cloves, finely grated
   or minced
1 tbsp gochujang
1 tbsp light soy sauce, plus
   extra to taste if needed
1 tbsp toasted sesame oil
1 tbsp sugar, plus extra to taste
   if needed
500ml vegetable stock
1 spring onion, finely sliced
Rice vinegar and honey, to
   taste if needed
Sprinkle of toasted white
   sesame seeds
Cooked sushi rice, to
   serve (optional)

This recipe takes inspiration from Korean *kimchi jjigae* (kimchi stew) and *sundubu jjigae* (spicy soft tofu stew). Its beauty lies in its balance – savoury, spicy, tangy and a little sweet, all at once. This is one of those dishes I come back to time and again when I want something warming and deeply satisfying.

The method couldn't be simpler. All the stew ingredients go straight into the pot – there's no sautéing or need for regular stirring – then it's just a 10-minute simmer before the tofu goes in. I've used firm tofu here because it holds its shape while staying tender, but extra-firm works just as well, if you prefer a bit more bite. In that case, it doesn't need pressing – just pat it dry and slice.

1 Drain the tofu and wrap it loosely in kitchen paper or a clean tea towel. Set it on a plate and rest a heavy chopping board on top. Leave it to press while you start the stew – this will both draw out excess moisture that would otherwise dilute the broth and help the tofu soak up more flavour.

2 Add the kimchi, tomatoes, onion, garlic, gochujang, soy sauce, sesame oil, sugar and vegetable stock to a large, wide sauté pan or pot. Bring the liquid to the boil over a high heat and stir everything together, then cover with a lid, reduce the heat to medium–high and cook for 10 minutes.

3 When there are a few minutes left, unwrap the tofu and slice it into 1cm-thick pieces.

4 Give the stew a stir, then gently lay the tofu on top (it's absolutely fine if it overlaps). Cover and cook for 10 minutes.

5 Carefully transfer the tofu to a large bowl or serving dish – as it's very delicate, it might break apart (no stress if it does).

6 The beauty of the broth lies in its balance, so taste it and adjust as needed. For more saltiness, add light soy sauce or a pinch of salt; for more tang, stir in a splash of rice vinegar; for extra sweetness, add a touch of sugar or honey. Pour the broth over the tofu and finish with the spring onion and sesame seeds. Serve hot – with rice if you like, too.

Sticky Gochujang Sausages

Serves 4

1 tbsp vegetable oil (or
   any neutral oil)
36 raw cocktail sausages
3 tbsp runny honey
1 tbsp gochujang

Do these count as a proper dinner? No. But they're exactly the kind of thing I want as part of a picky tea. Sweet, spicy and gloriously sticky, they're quick to make, impossible to stop eating and perfect alongside a pile of crisps, bread and butter and whatever else you've pulled out of the fridge.

1 Heat your oven to 200°C/180°C fan. Add the oil to a medium roasting tin and heat it up in the oven for 5 minutes. Carefully tip the sausages into the hot oil and toss them to coat.

2 Bake the sausages, for 20–25 minutes, tossing them halfway through, until browned and cooked through.

3 Meanwhile, mix together the honey and gochujang to make a glaze.

4 Once the sausages are cooked, drain them on some kitchen paper, then return them to the roasting tin. Add the gochujang honey glaze and toss the sausages to coat them evenly.

5 Return the tin to the oven for a further 5 minutes, turning the sausages halfway through, until sticky all over. Serve hot or warm with cocktail sticks for picking.

Lao-Inspired Crispy Rice Salad

Serves 2

3 tbsp vegetable oil (or
  any neutral oil)
1 tbsp good-quality Thai
  red curry paste (see note,
  page 60)
2 tsp runny honey or
  agave nectar
250g cold cooked jasmine rice
4 tbsp rice flour or cornflour

For the dressing
4 tbsp lime juice
2 tbsp fish sauce (or vegan
  fish sauce)
1–2 tbsp caster sugar, to taste
1 red chilli, finely chopped
  (deseed for less heat)

For the salad
60g roasted peanuts, roughly
  chopped
½ red onion, very thinly sliced
2 spring onions, thinly sliced
1 small handful of fresh
  coriander, leaves and tender
  stems finely chopped

To serve (optional)
2 fried eggs
2 baby or little gem lettuces,
  leaves separated

This is my take on *nam khao*, the Lao crispy rice salad that's all about contrast – crunch and chew, heat and sourness, depth and freshness. Here, instead of shaping and deep-frying rice balls, you toss rice in Thai red curry paste and honey (or agave), then roast it until golden and crispy. The rest is all about layering: peanuts for crunch, herbs for freshness, chilli for heat and a sharp, salty-sour dressing to tie it all together. I like to serve it with a crispy fried egg on top, but it also works great on its own with baby or little gem leaves for scooping, or alongside some grilled fish or meat.

1 Heat your oven to 220°C/200°C fan. Line a medium roasting tin with baking paper.

2 In a medium mixing bowl, whisk together the vegetable oil, Thai red curry paste and honey or agave nectar.

3 Add the cooked jasmine rice, season lightly with salt, and toss, ensuring that all the grains are evenly coated. Add the rice flour or cornflour and toss well again to coat.

4 Transfer the rice mixture to the prepared roasting tin and spread it out into an even layer. Bake for 20–25 minutes, tossing once halfway through, or until nice and crispy.

5 While the rice is in the oven, mix the dressing ingredients in a large bowl (now would be a good time to prep the salad ingredients too, if you haven't already).

6 Once the rice is crispy, add it to the dressing, along with the salad ingredients – the roasted peanuts, red onion, spring onions and coriander. Toss to combine, and serve immediately – on its own, topped with a fried egg, with gem lettuce leaves for scooping, or alongside some grilled fish or meat.

Smoky Tuna Tostadas

Serves 4

4–8 small corn tortillas
Vegetable oil (or any
 neutral oil)
60g mayonnaise
1 tsp chipotle paste
50ml lime juice
50ml light soy sauce
230g sushi-grade tuna, cut
 into 3mm slices (about the
 thickness of a £1 coin)
1 avocado, stoned, peeled and
 thinly sliced
2 spring onions, very
 thinly sliced
Lime wedges, to serve

Now, this one's more of a snack or starter than a full-blown dinner, but it had to make the cut – it's just too good! The recipe is inspired by the tuna tostadas I had at Contramar in Mexico City, which are the best I've ever tasted. They had this incredible smoky depth, a bold hit of allium and *just* the right balance of freshness and richness. I wanted to capture those flavours, but in a more straightforward and home-kitchen-friendly kind of way. Crisp corn tostadas form the base, topped with marinated tuna, smoky chipotle mayo, avocado and lots of spring onions. They're simple but so, *so* good.

1 Heat your oven to 200°C/180°C fan. Lightly brush both sides of each tortilla with a little vegetable oil and arrange them in a single layer on a baking tray. Bake for 8–12 minutes, flipping halfway, or until crisp, and golden on both sides. Transfer the tortillas to a wire rack – they will crisp up further as they cool.

2 In a small bowl, mix together the mayonnaise and chipotle paste until well combined.

3 In a separate bowl, mix the lime juice and soy sauce, then add the tuna and toss gently to coat. Leave the fish to marinate for 5 minutes, then drain off any excess liquid.

4 Spread a little chipotle mayo over each tostada. Top with a few slices of tuna, followed by the avocado. Season the avocado with a tiny pinch of salt, then finish the tostadas with a sprinkle of spring onions. Serve immediately with lime wedges on the side.

Lemongrass & Coconut Seafood Soup

Serves 4

1 x 400g tin of good-quality coconut milk (at least 70% coconut extract)

400ml vegetable stock

2 lemongrass stalks, bruised with a rolling pin or pestle

50g fresh ginger, peeled and sliced

2 limes, zest (save the limes for squeezing to serve)

2 red chillies, 1 halved, 1 thinly sliced (deseeded for less heat)

1 tbsp fish sauce

1 tsp light brown soft sugar

300g deveined, peeled raw king prawns

150g oyster or shiitake mushrooms, thinly sliced

10g fresh coriander, leaves and tender stems finely chopped

Steamed jasmine rice, to serve

Fragrant, creamy and full of flavour, this soup is pure comfort in a bowl. The broth is fragrant with lemongrass and ginger, and the coconut milk adds just the right amount of richness without making the soup heavy. I've used raw king prawns here, but you could easily swap in a fish-pie mixture or thawed frozen raw seafood medley. Enjoy this soup as is, or with rice to soak up all that delicious broth.

*This recipe works really well with **vegan alternatives**. Simply swap the fish sauce for light soy sauce and replace the prawns with a cubed firm tofu.*

1   Pour the coconut milk and vegetable stock into a medium saucepan, then add the lemongrass, ginger, lime zest, halved red chilli, fish sauce and sugar. Stir to combine.

2   Bring the liquid to a gentle simmer over a medium-high heat, then reduce the heat to low, cover and cook for 20 minutes to let the flavours infuse.

3   Once the broth has been bubbling for 20 minutes, gently stir in the prawns and mushrooms, then turn the heat up to medium-high. Bring the soup back to a gentle simmer, then lower the heat again to medium and cook for 2–3 minutes, or until the prawns are just cooked through and the mushrooms have softened.

4   Remove the pan from the heat, then stir in the thinly sliced red chilli and the coriander. Divide the soup equally between your serving bowls and serve with lime wedges on the side for squeezing. Enjoy as is or with a side of steamed rice to soak up that delicious broth.

45 Minutes

There's something so satisfying about the pace of a 45-minute cook. It gives you enough time to build depth, layer flavours and settle into the kind of rhythm that makes the process of cooking itself enjoyable.

My goal in sharing recipes online has always been to help people find joy in cooking. These recipes give you just enough time to tap into the rhythm – and, by extension, into what can make cooking so fun, therapeutic, gratifying and rewarding. There's time to slowly cook down aromatics for broths with real depth, to properly bloom spices for layered sauces and to coax more flavour from simple ingredients – such as mushrooms or onions, for example – just by letting them cook a little longer.

Some of my favourite recipes include the Caramelised Mushroom Shawarma, where spiced mushrooms are roasted until deeply golden while you throw together a punchy pomegranate salad and quick garlic yoghurt to go with them. Then there's my viral Coconut Milk Poached Fish, gently simmered in a broth infused with lemongrass, ginger, garlic and chilli. And finally, the Gochujang Hot Honey Chicken Katsu, a Korean twist on the Japanese classic, which pairs crispy chicken with a sweet, spicy glaze and a crunchy sesame slaw. Yes, these recipes take a little more time, but that's time enough to enjoy the rhythm. The results are worth it.

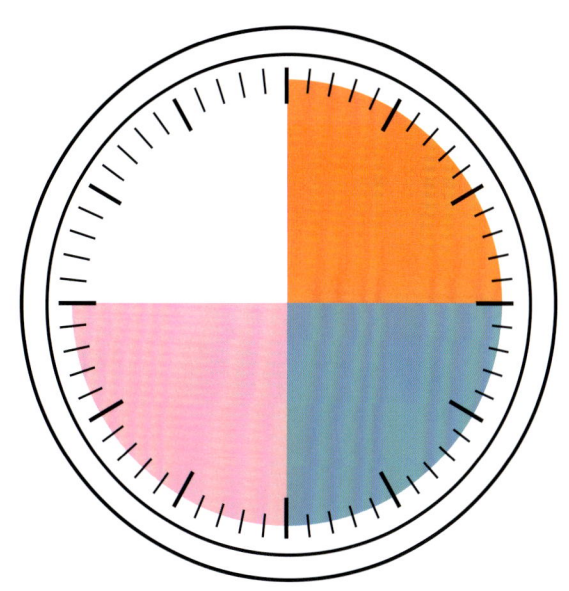

In this chapter

Coconut Milk Poached Fish

Serves 4

4 cod loins or fillets (about
  150g each), or any flaky white
  fish (skin on or off is fine)
2 lemongrass stalks, tough
  outer layers removed
1 onion
4 garlic cloves, peeled
15g fresh ginger, peeled
1 red chilli (optional; deseed for
  less heat)
Vegetable or coconut oil
2 × 400g tins of good-quality
  coconut milk (at least 70%
  coconut extract)
2 tbsp fish sauce
1 vegetable stock pot
1 tsp sugar
1 spring onion, thinly sliced
1 small handful of fresh
  coriander, leaves and tender
  stems finely chopped

To serve (optional)
Chilli oil
Cooked jasmine rice
Lime wedges

This is one of the most popular recipes on my blog, and once you taste the broth, you'll understand why. Inspired by some of my favourite Southeast Asian flavours, coconut milk gently simmers with aromatics like lemongrass, ginger, garlic and chillies, creating the most delicious, fragrant broth for poaching the cod fillets.

If you're nervous about cooking fish, poaching is a brilliant place to start. It's gentle and very forgiving. Here, it keeps the cod beautifully tender while the fish absorbs all that flavour from the liquid. You don't need to fuss – just let the broth do the work.

1   Season the cod fillets with salt on both sides, then refrigerate them for 30 minutes. This both seasons the cod and firms up its flesh, making it less likely to fall apart during poaching.

2   Meanwhile, roughly chop the lemongrass, onion, garlic, ginger and chilli (if using), then blitz them in a food processor until finely chopped.

3   Heat a tablespoon or two of vegetable or coconut oil in a medium sauté pan over a medium heat. Add the chopped aromatics, season with salt and pepper and cook gently, stirring occasionally, for 5 minutes, or until softened.

4   Add the coconut milk, fish sauce, stock pot and sugar. Season again with salt and pepper and stir to combine. Bring the broth to a simmer over a medium–high heat, then cover, reduce the heat to low or medium–low and leave to gently bubble for 25–30 minutes.

5   Nestle the cod into the broth, then put the lid on the pan and poach the fish for 5–8 minutes, depending on the thickness of the fillets. The fish is done when it flakes easily when gently pressed.

6   To serve, carefully lift the cod into shallow bowls and ladle over the broth. Top with the spring onion and coriander and finish with a drizzle of chilli oil (if using). I like to serve this with rice (it soaks up all of that delicious coconut broth), a side of steamed veg and a few lime wedges for squeezing over.

Creamy 'Nduja Risotto

Serves 6 (with leftovers for arancini!)

1.2 litres good-quality
  chicken stock
2 tbsp double-concentrate
  tomato purée
2 tbsp extra-virgin olive oil
1 onion, very finely chopped
80g 'nduja
2 garlic cloves, finely grated
  or minced
400g arborio or carnaroli rice
120ml dry white wine
100g parmigiano
  reggiano, grated
50g mascarpone
2 tbsp butter

Risotto is one of my all-time favourite things to make. It's very hands-on, requiring near constant stirring, but that's exactly what I love about it. The process is relaxing, almost meditative – perfect for getting out of your head after a long day. This risotto gets a big boost of flavour from 'nduja, a soft, spicy sausage from Calabria in southern Italy. Flavour-wise, it's salty, smoky and a little funky (the good kind!). It adds huge depth, transforming a simple risotto into something really special.

1 Pour the stock into a saucepan, whisk in the tomato purée and bring the liquid to a simmer over a medium heat. Reduce the heat to low, cover and keep warm.

2 Meanwhile, heat the olive oil in a large cast-iron casserole (Dutch oven) or sauté pan over a medium heat. Add the onion with a generous pinch of salt and cook, stirring occasionally, until softened but not coloured (around 5 minutes).

3 Add the 'nduja, breaking it up with a wooden spoon. It will begin to melt into the onions. Once fully softened, add the garlic and cook, stirring frequently, for 1 minute.

4 Stir in the rice, coating it in the 'nduja-y oil. Season with salt and pepper, then cook, stirring often, until the rice is lightly toasted (around 2–3 minutes).

5 Pour in the white wine and let it bubble away, stirring occasionally, until almost fully evaporated.

6 Start adding the hot stock, one ladleful at a time, stirring constantly and adding more only once the previous ladleful has been fully absorbed. Keep going until the rice is tender but still has a slight bite – this should take around 25–30 minutes. If you run out of stock before the rice is done, continue with ladlefuls of hot water until you reach the right consistency.

7 Add the parmigiano reggiano, mascarpone and butter, stirring until the butter is melted and fully incorporated. Remove the pan from the heat, cover and leave the risotto to sit for 3–5 minutes – this is where the magic happens, giving you the creamiest risotto possible. Taste and adjust the salt level to your liking, then serve.

Saffron Lamb Kebabs

Serves 4

½ tsp saffron threads
1 tbsp hot water
1 onion
500g lamb mince (15-20% fat;
  or use beef mince, if you like)
1 tbsp melted butter
2 garlic cloves, finely grated
  or minced
1 tbsp double-concentrate
  tomato purée
½ tsp smoked paprika
½ tsp sumac
1 handful of fresh flat-leaf
  parsley, leaves and tender
  stems finely chopped,
  to garnish

For the tomato & onion salad

1 onion, very thinly sliced
1 lemon, juice
1 tsp sumac
6 vine tomatoes (about 450g),
  cut into thin wedges
3-4 tbsp extra-virgin olive oil

For the rice

¼ tsp saffron threads (optional)
½ tbsp hot water (optional, if
  you're using the saffron)
250g white basmati rice
350ml chicken stock

This is my take on Persian *kabāb koobideh* – some of the richest, juiciest and most delicious kofta kebabs you'll ever try. The key is using lamb mince with enough fat and really working the mixture until it's sticky and cohesive. Saffron brings warmth and depth, while a little butter ensures the kebabs stay exceptionally juicy. Served over saffron rice with a simple tomato and onion salad, it makes for an easy but impressive dinner.

If you don't have the time (or desire) to make rice and salad from scratch, you absolutely can serve the kebabs with microwavable packet rice. The pan juices left behind after grilling the lamb are packed with flavour and perfect for spooning over plain rice.

1 Grind the saffron to a fine powder using a pestle and mortar, then add the hot water and leave the saffron to steep for 5 minutes.

2 Coarsely grate the onion, then transfer it to a fine-mesh sieve. Use the back of a spoon to press out and discard as much liquid as possible, then add the onion to a large mixing bowl. Add the saffron water, lamb mince (or beef), butter, garlic, tomato purée, smoked paprika and sumac. Season well with salt and pepper, then mix thoroughly until the mixture is sticky and cohesive.

3 Shape the mixture into 8 logs (for lack of a better word) and arrange them on a plate. Refrigerate while you prepare the other components. If you have time, let them marinate for an hour – this helps develop flavour – but if not, no stress.

4 Heat your oven grill to its highest setting, then line a small baking tray with foil and place a wire rack on top.

5 For the salad, place the onion, lemon juice and sumac in a small bowl. Scrunch with your hand until the onion softens slightly, then add the tomatoes and extra-virgin olive oil. Season with salt and pepper, and toss to combine. Set aside until you're ready to serve.

6 If you're using the saffron in the rice, grind it to a powder, add the hot water and leave the saffron to steep for 5 minutes.

7 Wash the rice until the water runs clear, then drain it and transfer it to a medium saucepan. Add the chicken stock, and the saffron water (if using), season with salt and stir to combine. Bring the liquid to a simmer over a high heat, then reduce the heat to low, cover the pan and cook the rice for 12 minutes, until the liquid has been absorbed and the grains are tender. Remove the pan from the heat and leave the rice to steam with the lid on for another 5 minutes.

8 While the rice cooks, lightly oil the grill rack and arrange the kebabs on it in a single layer. Grill them for 12 minutes, turning halfway, or until browned and cooked through. You'll be left with lots of delicious juices in the tray – pour them into a bowl or gravy boat to serve alongside.

9 To serve, spoon the rice on to plates and place the kebabs on top. Drizzle over a little of the cooking juices and scatter the kebabs with some of the parsley. Serve the salad on the side, finished with the remaining parsley.

Caramelised Mushroom Shawarma

Serves 4

6 tbsp extra-virgin olive oil
1½ tbsp double-concentrate
    tomato purée
2 tbsp ras el hanout
800g oyster mushrooms, torn
    or sliced into 1cm strips
3 banana shallots (echalion),
    quartered lengthways

For the garlic yoghurt
200g Greek yoghurt (or
    vegan yoghurt to make this
    recipe plant-based)
1 large garlic clove, finely
    grated or minced

For the pomegranate salad
250g pomegranate seeds
1 large sweet-pointed (romano)
    pepper, deseeded and
    finely diced
150g baby cucumbers,
    finely diced
1 large banana shallot
    (echalion), finely chopped
1 handful of mint, leaves picked
    and thinly sliced
3 tbsp extra-virgin olive oil
½–1 lemon, juice, to taste
Warmed flatbreads, to serve

These charred, deeply savoury mushrooms are inspired by shawarma. They're tossed in ras el hanout, which is one of my all-time favourite spice blends. It's a one-ingredient flavour powerhouse, bringing warmth, depth and complexity, while enhancing the mushrooms' natural meaty flavour. As they roast, you throw together a lemony pomegranate salad and quick garlic yoghurt. Then it's just a matter of piling everything on to warm, fluffy flatbreads for an incredibly delicious dinner – perfect for when you've got friends coming round (or just for yourself!).

1   Heat your oven to 220°C/200°C fan.

2   In a large bowl, mix the olive oil, tomato purée and ras el hanout until well-combined. Add the mushrooms and shallots, season with salt and pepper and toss the mushrooms until well-coated. Spread them out in a single layer over a large baking tray (about 45cm × 33cm) or two medium trays. Roast the mushrooms for around 20 minutes, or until tender and browned.

3   Meanwhile, make the garlic yoghurt and salad. Mix the yoghurt with the garlic and a pinch of salt in a small bowl. Set aside. In another bowl, combine all the pomegranate salad ingredients, season with salt and pepper and toss to combine.

4   I like to serve this DIY shawarma-style, with all the components laid out so everyone can build their own wraps.

Beer-Battered Fish Tacos

Serves 4

4 cod loins (about 125g each)
3–4 tbsp plain flour
Vegetable oil (or any neutral oil), for deep-frying

For the slaw
½ white cabbage, very thinly sliced
½ onion, very thinly sliced
1 jalapeño, very thinly sliced
2 limes, juice (or more, to taste)

For the batter
130g plain flour
30g cornflour
1 tsp chipotle, ancho or regular chilli powder
1 tsp baking powder
1 tsp fine sea salt
250ml fridge-cold beer

For the avocado crema
1 large avocado
100g soured cream
10g fresh coriander

To serve
12 small corn or flour tortillas
Optional: thinly sliced red chilli, lime wedges and hot honey

This is everything I want in a fish taco: crispy, golden beer-battered cod, a bright, zingy slaw and a smooth avocado crema to bring it all together. I won't lie, this is one of the – if not the most – labour-intensive recipes in this book, but I promise you, these tacos are worth it! The slaw makes more than you need, but I like serving extra on the side.

1   Start with the slaw. Combine the cabbage, onion, jalapeño and lime juice in a bowl. Season well with salt and pepper and toss to coat. Put the slaw in the fridge while you prep everything else. It will look and feel a little dry at this stage but don't worry – it'll soften as it sits.

2   Fill a large sauté pan or cast-iron casserole (Dutch oven) halfway with vegetable oil and heat it over a medium–high heat until it reaches 180°C. If you don't have a thermometer, dip the handle of a wooden spoon into the hot oil – the oil will bubble rapidly around the handle when it's ready for frying.

3   Meanwhile, pat the cod loins dry with kitchen paper and slice each into six strips. Season the strips with salt and pepper, then dust them with the plain flour and toss gently to coat. You can do this directly on your chopping board.

4   To make the batter, in a medium mixing bowl, whisk together the plain flour, cornflour, chilli powder, baking powder and salt. Add the cold beer and whisk until just combined – a few lumps are fine.

5   Working in batches, dip each piece of floured cod into the batter. Let the excess drip off and fry each batch for 4 minutes, or until the pieces are golden and crisp. Transfer the cod to a wire rack to drain.

6   While the fish cools slightly, make the crema. Peel and stone the avocado, then add the flesh to a blender with the soured cream, coriander, 1–2 tablespoons of water and a good pinch of salt until smooth. I like making this last to keep the colour nice and vibrant.

7   Warm your tortillas according to the package instructions.

8   To assemble, spread a spoonful of avocado crema on to each tortilla. Add some slaw, followed by one or two pieces of fried cod. Top with a few slices of red chilli (if using) and serve with lime wedges on the side, if you like. A little rogue, but I love a drizzle of hot honey to finish.

Golden Thai Curry Chicken Noodle Soup

(Or 30 minutes, if you don't make the crispy chicken skin)

Serves 2

1 heaped tbsp good-quality Thai red curry paste (see note, page 60)
1 tbsp fish sauce
1½ tbsp palm sugar or light brown soft sugar
1 tsp ground turmeric
1 × 400g tin of good-quality coconut milk (70% or more coconut extract)
400ml chicken stock
10g fresh ginger, finely grated or minced
2 skin-on, bone-in chicken thighs
2 portions of ramen noodles (dried, fresh or frozen – I prefer frozen for the texture, and they boil in just 1 minute)
1 large handful of beansprouts
1 small handful of fresh coriander, leaves and tender stems roughly chopped
Chilli oil, for drizzling (optional)

When I first shared this recipe, the internet went wild for it. Once you try it, you'll see why. It's hearty, comforting and bursting with flavour. The star of the show is the umami-packed broth, which comes together in just 20 minutes. Its strength is entirely dependent on the quality of the curry paste you use, so go for one made with natural, authentic Thai ingredients.

Bone-in chicken thighs have a depth of flavour that's great for this dish – you get so much from cooking meat on the bone. That said, boneless, skinless thighs work too, and drumsticks are also a solid option. I would avoid chicken breasts, though, as they'll dry out too quickly in this kind of broth.

1 Add the curry paste, fish sauce, sugar, turmeric, coconut milk, chicken stock and ginger to a medium saucepan. Season with a good pinch of salt and whisk to combine.

2 Remove the skin from the chicken thighs (save it if you want to make a crispy skin topping) and add the thighs to the broth. Bring the liquid to the boil over a medium–high heat, then lower the heat to medium–low, cover, and simmer for 15 minutes, or until the chicken is cooked through.

3 If you are making the crispy skin topping, heat the oven 180°C/160°C fan. Place the chicken skins top-side down on a chopping board and scrape off any excess fat using a small knife. Lay the skins on a lined baking tray, cover with another sheet of baking paper and weigh them down with a heavy tray or pan on top. Bake for 25–30 minutes, or until golden and crisp. Set aside.

4 Once the chicken thighs are cooked, lift them out of the broth with tongs and set them aside to cool slightly. Remove the meat from the bones and chop it into bite-sized pieces.

5 Boil the noodles in well-salted water according to the package instructions. Drain them, and divide them equally between two serving bowls.

6 Top the noodles with the chopped chicken, ladle over the broth, and finish with the beansprouts, coriander, and chilli oil (if using).

Charred Hispi Cabbage with Cheat's Labneh

Serves 4

½ tsp fine sea salt
225g thick Greek yoghurt
  (it needs to be thick!)
1 sweetheart cabbage (aka
  sweet pointed or hispi
  cabbage), quartered
  lengthways through the core
2 tbsp extra-virgin olive oil,
  plus more for drizzling
½ tbsp ras el hanout
½ tsp garlic granules
  or powder
Dukkah, to garnish

Cabbage gets an unfairly bad rap. It's affordable, incredibly versatile and absolutely delicious when cooked well. Charring it brings out its natural sweetness and gives it the most beautiful nutty flavour. What makes this charred cabbage so special is the garlicky ras el hanout oil it's brushed with.

I've said it elsewhere in this book, but ras el hanout is one of my favourite spice blends of all time (see page 11). With its bold, complex flavour, it does all of the heavy lifting, keeping this recipe nice and simple. The cabbage gets charred and roasted until tender, before being served over a quick cheat's labneh made with nothing but Greek yoghurt and salt. A final sprinkle of dukkah adds crunch and brings it all together.

1   Heat your oven to 200°C/180°C fan.

2   Line a sieve with a clean cloth and set it over a bowl. Stir the salt into the Greek yoghurt, then transfer the yoghurt to the cloth and squeeze gently to remove some liquid. Weigh it down with something heavy and refrigerate for 30–40 minutes to strain further. The extra-thickened yoghurt left in the cloth is your cheat's labneh.

3   Meanwhile, drizzle the cabbage quarters with a little olive oil, season generously with salt and rub the leaves to coat.

4   Heat a large, heavy frying pan over a high heat and sear the cabbage pieces, cut-side down, for 4–5 minutes, or until deeply charred. Flip and sear the other cut side for 4–5 minutes, or until charred, then transfer the cabbage pieces to a roasting tin cut-side up.

5   Mix the olive oil with the ras el hanout, garlic granules or powder and a pinch of salt and pepper. Brush this over the cabbage wedges and roast for 25 minutes, or until tender.

6   Spread the cheat's labneh on to a serving plate, top with the charred cabbage wedges and finish with a sprinkle of dukkah.

Crispy Prawn Burgers

Makes 2 burgers

165g deveined, peeled raw
  king prawns
1 tsp garlic and ginger paste
  (or ½ tsp each of garlic paste
  and ginger paste)
3 tbsp mayonnaise
1–3 tsp sriracha, to taste
  (depending on how much
  heat you enjoy)
20g plain flour
1 large egg, beaten
50g panko breadcrumbs
Vegetable oil (or any neutral
  oil), for shallow-frying
Flaky salt, for sprinkling
2 brioche burger buns, halved
  through the middle
4 baby gem lettuce leaves

I rarely make burgers at home, but when I do I like to go all out. These are truly sensational – they're all about letting the prawns shine. The patties aren't bulked out with breadcrumbs or starch, and there's no egg either – just prawns, garlic and ginger. You blitz half to form a paste that holds everything together, and leave the rest chunky to keep some texture and stop the patties becoming heavy.

The patties are coated in panko, shallow-fried until golden and crisp, then layered into toasted brioche buns with crunchy lettuce and sriracha mayo. Indulgent and delicious – perfect for a fakeaway treat.

1 Roughly chop half the prawns and tip them into a bowl.

2 Add the remaining, whole prawns to a food processor with the garlic and ginger paste. Pulse to a chunky paste, then scrape this into the bowl with the chopped prawns. Season well with salt and pepper and mix to combine. With damp hands, shape the mixture into two 10cm patties and place them on a plate lined with baking paper. Freeze the patties for 10–15 minutes to firm up slightly.

3 In the meantime, mix the mayonnaise and sriracha to make the burger sauce. Keep it in the fridge until needed.

4 Set up your dredging station with three shallow bowls: one with the flour, one with the beaten egg (seasoned with a pinch of salt and pepper) and one with the panko breadcrumbs.

5 Remove the chilled patties from the freezer and coat each one in flour, then egg, then panko, making sure they're evenly covered. The patties will still be a little soft – take your time and handle them gently.

6 Heat 2–3cm of oil in a sauté pan over a high heat. Once shimmering, fry the patties for 2–3 minutes on each side, or until golden, crispy and springy to the touch. Transfer them to a plate lined with kitchen paper to drain, and sprinkle with a little flaky salt.

7 Lightly toast the brioche buns in a dry pan (cut-sides down) or under a hot grill (cut-sides up). To assemble, spread some of the spicy mayo over the bottom bun halves. Add the baby gem leaves, then the prawn burgers. Spoon over more sauce and close with the top of the buns. Serve immediately.

Mapo Aubergine

Serves 4

2 aubergines
1 tbsp vegetable oil (or any
   neutral oil)
4 large garlic cloves, finely
   grated or minced
25g fresh ginger, finely grated
   or minced
2 spring onions, thinly sliced,
   whites and greens separated
250g pork mince (or
   beef, lamb, chicken or
   plant-based mince)
1 tsp Sichuan
   peppercorns, ground
1½ tbsp spicy bean sauce
1 tbsp Shaoxing wine
400ml chicken stock (or
   vegetable stock)
1 tbsp chilli oil
2 tsp light soy sauce
1 tsp toasted sesame oil
2 tsp sugar
1 tbsp cornflour, mixed with
   2 tbsp water
Cooked white basmati rice,
   to serve

If you think you hate aubergine, think again – this recipe might just convert you. Here, it stands in for tofu in a take on Chinese mapo tofu born of my family's firm (and unfortunate) aversion to the stuff. It's not traditional, but it still captures the soul of mapo tofu: it's packed with *mála* – hot, numbing flavour – from fermented spicy bean sauce and Sichuan peppercorns.

Back to my claim about converting you to aubergine. This humble vegetable gets a bad rap for being rubbery and squeaky, but – I'll be frank – that usually comes down to how it's cooked. The key to making aubergines delicious is cooking them for longer than you think. Here, they're first dry roasted – without any oil or seasoning – before being simmered in the delicious sauce, which makes them silky, rich and packed with flavour.

Spicy bean sauce is a fermented paste made with broad beans and chilli, often used in Sichuan cooking to add deep, savoury heat (take care with the amount – 1½ tablespoons is enough; any more can make the dish too salty). You'll sometimes see it labelled as Ma Po Sauce, especially in supermarkets. It's closely related to chilli bean sauce (doubanjiang or toban djan), but typically a little smoother, slightly sweeter and less pungent. Spicy bean sauce is key to the flavour of mapo tofu, but it's also great for adding richness and spice to stir-fries, noodles and marinades. You can find it in larger supermarkets with a decent world-food section or in Chinese or East Asian food shops, or online.

1 Heat your oven to 220°C/200°C fan and line a large roasting tin with baking paper.

2 Slice the aubergines on a diagonal into 1.5cm-thick pieces, then arrange them in a single layer over the baking paper and roast them for 20 minutes – no oil, no seasoning (trust the process!). While the aubergine roasts, you can prep the remaining ingredients, if you haven't already.

3 About 10 minutes before the aubergine is done, heat the oil in a large wok or frying pan over a medium heat. Add the garlic, ginger and spring-onion whites and stir-fry for 1 minute, or until fragrant.

continued overleaf . . .

4 Turn the heat up to high, add the pork (or other) mince and break it up with your spatula or wooden spoon. Stir-fry for 3–5 minutes, or until starting to brown.

5 Add the Sichuan peppercorns and spicy bean sauce and stir-fry for 1 minute, then add the Shaoxing wine and scrape up any browned bits from the bottom of the pan.

6 Add the stock, chilli oil, soy sauce, sesame oil and sugar, then stir through the roasted aubergine.

7 Bring the liquid to the boil, then cover the pot with a lid and simmer the sauce over a medium or medium–low heat for 10 minutes.

8 Stir the cornflour slurry into the pot and cook for another 1 minute with the lid off to thicken the sauce. Serve hot, topped with spring-onion greens. I like it with plenty of steamed white basmati rice.

Gochujang Hot Honey Chicken Katsu

Serves 4

650g boneless, skinless
  chicken thighs
65g plain flour
2 tsp fine sea salt
2 tsp garlic granules or powder
2 tsp onion granules
  or powder
2 large eggs
150g panko breadcrumbs
Vegetable oil (or any neutral
  oil), for shallow-frying
Flaky salt, for sprinkling

For the sesame cabbage
½ sweetheart cabbage (aka
  sweet pointed or hispi
  cabbage), very thinly sliced
2 tbsp toasted sesame oil
2 tbsp toasted sesame seeds

For the gochujang hot honey
100g runny honey
½ tbsp gochujang
1 garlic clove, finely grated
  or minced

To serve
1 lime, cut into wedges,
  for squeezing

I don't know about you, but when I think of fried chicken, my mind never goes to chicken katsu – which is strange, given that it's one of my favourite Japanese dishes. Maybe it's because it's so good that it exists in my mind in a realm of its own? Who knows. This recipe puts a bit of a Korean twist on things, swapping the usual tonkatsu sauce for a garlicky gochujang hot honey. It's so incredibly delicious and pairs beautifully with the sesame cabbage slaw, which brings some much-needed freshness. As does the bright, zingy lime.

1   Make the sesame cabbage. In a large bowl, combine the cabbage, sesame oil and sesame seeds. Season with salt and pepper and toss well to coat, then refrigerate until you're ready to serve. It'll look and feel a little dry at this stage but don't worry – it'll soften as it sits.

2   Use a rolling pin or meat mallet to gently pound the chicken thigh fillets to an even thickness of around 1.5cm. Set up your dredging station. First, in a wide, shallow bowl, mix the flour, salt, and garlic and onion granules (or powder) until well combined. Crack the eggs into a separate wide, shallow bowl, season lightly with salt and pepper and whisk to combine. Finally, tip the panko into a wide, shallow bowl.

3   Working one thigh at a time, dredge the chicken in the seasoned flour, then shake off the excess and dip it into the egg. Turn to coat, letting the excess drip back into the bowl, then transfer to the panko. Press the chicken into the breadcrumbs to fully coat and adhere.

4   Fill a large sauté pan or cast-iron casserole (Dutch oven) with 2–3cm of vegetable oil and set the pan over a high heat. Wait until the oil is shimmering hot, then, working in batches, fry the chicken for 3 minutes per side, or until golden and crispy (adjust the heat if the breadcrumbs are browning too quickly). Transfer the cooked chicken to a plate lined with kitchen paper and sprinkle with flaky salt. Keep warm in a low oven while you cook the remaining fillets.

5   To make the hot honey, combine the honey, gochujang and garlic with a pinch of salt in a small saucepan. Set the pan over a medium heat and bring the mixture to a gentle simmer – just until the sauce is glossy and pourable. Remove from the heat.

6   Slice the katsu into strips and spoon over as much gochujang hot honey as you like. Serve with the sesame cabbage and lime wedges.

Creamy Gochujang Tomato Soup with Kimchi Cheese Toasties

Serves 4

1kg cherry or baby plum
   tomatoes, halved (see note,
   page 24)
2 red sweet-pointed (romano)
   peppers, deseeded and cut
   into 2-3cm chunks
1 onion, cut into eighths
6 garlic cloves, peeled
50g fresh ginger, peeled
   and sliced
3 tbsp vegetable oil (or any
   neutral oil)
150ml single cream
1 tbsp gochujang
1 tbsp light soy sauce

For the toasties
Butter, for spreading
8 slices of white bread
100g drained kimchi (see note,
   page 34)
120g grated mozzarella

Tomato soup and a cheese toastie is a classic combination for good reason. It's warm, cosy and does the job on cold nights when nothing else quite will. This version puts a Korean twist on things, with a spoonful of gochujang stirred through the soup for heat, depth and umami. Served alongside gooey kimchi and mozzarella toasties, it makes for a rich, satisfying, comforting – and exciting – meal.

1 Heat your oven to 220°C/200°C fan.

2 Place the tomatoes, peppers, onion, garlic, ginger and oil in a 35cm × 25cm roasting tin. Season with salt and pepper, toss to combine and roast for 30 minutes, until the tomatoes have slumped and the peppers and onion are tender. I recommend setting a timer (you'll refer to it later in the recipe).

3 Meanwhile, prep the toasties. Butter one side of all 8 slices of bread. Place 4 slices butter-side down on a sheet of baking paper. Top these with the kimchi (25g per toastie), spreading it out evenly, then scatter over the grated mozzarella (30g per toastie). Top with the remaining bread slices, buttered-side up.

4 When there are 10 minutes left on the roasting timer, place a large baking tray in the oven to preheat.

5 Take the roasting tin and preheated tray out of the oven. Carefully transfer the toasties from the baking paper to the hot tray, arranging them in a single layer. Bake, flipping halfway through, for 10-12 minutes, or until golden on both sides and the cheese is melted.

6 Meanwhile, tip the roasted veg (and all the juices) into a blender. Add the single cream, gochujang and soy sauce and blend until smooth.

7 Pour the blended soup into a saucepan, bring it to a simmer over a medium–high heat, then turn the heat to medium–low, cover the pan with a lid, and simmer for 5 minutes. Taste and adjust the seasoning with salt and pepper, if needed. Ladle the soup into bowls and serve with the hot toasties on the side.

One-Pan Harissa Chicken & Rice

Serves 4

¼ tsp saffron threads
1 tbsp hot water
650g boneless chicken thighs
   (skin on or off)
2 tbsp harissa paste
1 tsp ground cumin
1 tsp ground coriander
350g basmati rice
1 tbsp vegetable oil
1 onion, thinly sliced
2 garlic cloves, finely chopped
500ml chicken stock

To serve

100g natural yoghurt
½ lemon, juice
1 small handful of fresh flat-leaf
   parsley, leaves and tender
   stems roughly chopped

The key to creating deeply delicious one-pan meals is building layers of flavour. While it might be tempting to throw everything in at once, taking a few extra minutes to add ingredients in stages gives you so much more depth – it's the difference between a good meal and a great one. Here, you season chicken with harissa and warm spices, then give it a quick sear. This creates a flavourful fond to cook the onion and garlic, which in turn forms a rich, savoury base for toasting the rice. The latter then soaks up the saffron and stock, cooking alongside the spiced chicken. Finish with a spoonful of lemony yoghurt to cool everything down and you've got a deeply satisfying one-pan dinner.

1   Grind the saffron to a powder using a pestle and mortar, then add the hot water and set aside for 5 minutes to steep.

2   In a large bowl, combine the chicken thighs with the harissa paste, ground cumin and ground coriander. Season with salt and pepper and toss well to coat, then leave the thighs to marinate while you rinse the rice until the water runs clear. Set the rice aside to drain.

3   Heat the oil in a large sauté pan or cast-iron casserole (Dutch oven) over a medium–high heat. Sear the chicken in batches for 2–3 minutes per side, or until lightly browned (being careful not to let the harissa burn), transferring them to a plate as you go. The chicken won't be cooked through at this stage – it'll finish cooking with the rice.

4   Add the onion and cook, stirring occasionally, for 3 minutes, or until it is beginning to soften, then add the garlic and cook, stirring frequently, for 1 minute. Add the drained rice and toast it in the pan with the onion and garlic, stirring occasionally, for 2 minutes, then pour in the saffron water and stock.

5   Nestle the chicken into the rice and bring everything to a simmer. Reduce the heat to low, cover the pan with a lid and cook for 20–25 minutes, or until the rice is tender and the liquid has been absorbed.

6   To serve, mix the yoghurt with the lemon juice and season with salt and pepper. Serve this spooned over the chicken and rice (or on the side), with a scattering of parsley to finish.

Celebration Crab Curry

Serves 4

2 tbsp coconut oil

1 onion, finely chopped

2 large garlic cloves, thinly sliced

15g fresh ginger, peeled and thinly sliced

4 green cardamom pods, crushed

5g fresh curry leaves

200g brown crab meat

1½ tbsp medium curry powder

1 × 400g tin of good-quality coconut milk (at least 70% coconut extract)

500g white crab meat

½–1 lemon, juice, to taste

1 small handful of fresh coriander, leaves and tender stems finely chopped

Cooked white basmati rice and warmed naans or parathas, to serve

This isn't your everyday curry – it's a special-occasion curry. The kind I love making for friends and family when there's something to celebrate. But just because it feels celebratory doesn't mean it's complicated or labour-intensive. It comes together in just over 30 minutes – and tastes like it's been gently simmering for hours. That's largely down to the brown crab, which brings a rich, almost bisque-like depth, while the white meat stays sweet and delicate.

The base of the curry is nice and simple: just standard aromatics, medium curry powder – and fresh curry leaves, the star of the show. They add a warm, citrusy lift, while also providing a deeply savoury backbone. I like to serve this curry with basmati rice and naan or parathas, and I always finish everything with a big squeeze of lemon – it cuts through the richness and really makes the crab shine.

Fresh curry leaves are available in most South Asian food stores, and in some larger nationwide supermarkets. For me, there is no substitute. While the dried variety exists, the leaves lack the punch and freshness of their fresh counterpart – so much so that I don't think they're worth using at all.

1 Heat the coconut oil in a medium saucepan over a medium–low heat. Add the onion, garlic, ginger and cardamom, and cook, stirring occasionally, for 10 minutes, or until the onion has softened and is beginning to brown.

2 Turn the heat up to medium, then add the curry leaves and cook, stirring frequently, for 1 minute, until bright green and fragrant.

3 Add the brown crab meat and curry powder and cook, stirring frequently, for 2 minutes.

4 Add the coconut milk and 200ml of water, then season with salt and pepper. Stir to combine, and bring the liquid to a simmer. Cover the pan with a lid, turn the heat down to medium-low and cook, removing the lid to stir occasionally, for 10 minutes.

5 Stir in the white crab meat and simmer, covered, for 5 minutes, or until heated through. Remove the saucepan from the heat, then add the lemon juice to taste and stir through the coriander. Serve hot with basmati rice and naan or parathas.

Sweet Chilli Garlic Lime Wings

Serves 4

Vegetable oil (or other neutral oil), for greasing
1kg chicken wings, separated at the joint
2 tsp baking powder
½ tsp fine sea salt
150g sweet chilli sauce
4 garlic cloves, finely grated or minced
1 lime, zest and juice

There are good wings, and then there are *great* wings. These fall firmly into the latter category. Roasted to golden perfection, they're crispy on the outside and tender on the inside, all without the need for deep-frying. The glaze is simple but delicious: a mixture of sweet chilli sauce, garlic and fresh lime – the perfect blend of sweet, tangy and savoury.

Is it dinner in and of itself? I suppose that depends on who you ask. I've definitely had it as a meal on its own (though to be fair, I *love* chicken wings – so much so that I'd dedicate an entire cookbook to them were it commercially viable!). If not, they're the perfect thing to make as part of a picky tea: salad bits, crisps and whatever fridge-raided extras you've got knocking about.

Baking powder is the secret to super-crispy oven-baked wings. It raises the pH for better browning and draws out moisture, allowing the chicken to crisp up beautifully in the oven.

1 Heat your oven to 230°C/210°C fan. Line a large baking tray with foil for easy clean-up, then place a wire rack inside and oil it to prevent sticking. We'll be roasting the wings directly on the rack – this helps the air circulate around them, making them extra crispy.

2 Thoroughly pat the wing parts dry with kitchen paper (moisture is the enemy of crispiness!), then transfer the wings to a large mixing bowl. Add the baking powder and salt and toss well, ensuring that the wings are evenly coated.

3 Arrange the wings in a single layer on the oiled wire rack. Roast them for 20 minutes, then flip them and roast for a further 15–20 minutes until cooked through and thoroughly crispy.

4 Shortly before the wings are done, place the sweet chilli sauce, garlic, and lime zest and juice in a small saucepan. Bring the mixture to a simmer over a medium-high heat, then turn the heat down to low and simmer for 2 minutes to thicken.

5 Transfer the cooked wings to a large bowl. Add the sweet chilli glaze and toss to coat. Serve immediately.

Sticky Gochujang Tofu Congee

Serves 4

For the congee
1.2 litres vegetable stock
150g sushi rice
15g fresh ginger, peeled and
  thinly sliced

**For the sticky
gochujang sauce**
1 tbsp gochujang
1 tbsp light soy sauce
½–1 tbsp sugar, to taste
1 garlic clove, finely grated
  or minced

For the tofu
300g extra-firm tofu
1 tbsp cornflour
1 tbsp vegetable oil (or any
  neutral oil)
1 tbsp toasted sesame oil
1 tbsp toasted sesame seeds

To serve
2 spring onions, thinly sliced
Chilli oil, for drizzling (optional)

There are few things more comforting than a bowl of congee, with its gentle, creamy texture. Here, that familiar comfort gets a lively kick from tofu, pan-fried and tossed in a sticky-sweet, spicy gochujang glaze. It's an unusual pairing but it works really well. As cheesy as it sounds, it's a hug in a bowl, and perfect for cold winter nights.

1   Bring the vegetable stock to the boil in a large saucepan over a high heat (keep the lid on to speed things up). While you wait, rinse the sushi rice in cold water until the water runs clear, then leave to drain.

2   Once the stock is boiling, add the rice and ginger. Stir once, then bring everything back to the boil. Reduce the heat to medium and simmer the rice for 35 minutes with the lid slightly askew, until porridge-like. I recommend setting a timer for this (you'll refer back to it later in the recipe).

3   Meanwhile, in a small bowl make the sauce. Mix together the gochujang, soy sauce, sugar, garlic and 2 tablespoons of water. Set the sauce aside.

4   Around 10 minutes before the congee is done, pat the tofu dry, then crumble it into a large bowl in bite-sized chunks. Add the cornflour and toss to coat.

5   Heat the vegetable oil in a wok or large sauté pan over a medium-high heat. Add the tofu and stir-fry, tossing occasionally, for 6–8 minutes, or until lightly golden on all sides.

6   Pour in the gochujang sauce and stir it through. Let it bubble away for 1 minute, or until slightly thickened and sticky, then take the pan off the heat and stir in the sesame oil and seeds.

7   Once the congee timer is up, whisk the mixture vigorously for 2–3 minutes. It should be creamy and thick. Ladle the congee equally into your serving bowls and top with the sticky tofu. Finish with spring onions, and a drizzle of chilli oil, if you like.

Tarka Roasted Cauliflower

Serves 4

1 large cauliflower head
Extra-virgin olive oil
100g butter
2 tsp mustard seeds
2 tsp cumin seeds
4 garlic cloves, finely grated or
   minced
5cm piece of fresh ginger,
   finely grated or minced
30 fresh curry leaves (see
   note, page 143)
1 tsp mild Kashmiri
   chilli powder
5 tbsp Greek yoghurt
Warmed flatbreads, to serve

This is one of the most cooked recipes on my blog. It's packed with flavour and is so simple to make. Once you've seared and roasted the cauliflower, you make a quick, non-traditional brown-butter tarka, which gets poured over the top. Serve the dish with flatbreads to mop up that delicious sauce and you've got yourself a belter of a veggie dinnertime dish.

1 Heat your oven to 200°C/180°C fan.

2 Quarter the cauliflower, drizzle the pieces lightly with olive oil and season them generously with salt and pepper. Place a dry, ovenproof frying pan over a medium heat and, when hot, sear the cauliflower pieces, until browned on both cut sides (about 4 minutes per side). Transfer the pan to the oven and roast the cauliflower for 15 minutes, or until tender with a slight bite.

3 Meanwhile, melt the butter in a small saucepan over a medium heat. It'll bubble for a couple of minutes. As the bubbles subside, the milk solids will sink and begin to caramelise.

4 Once the butter smells nice and nutty, add the mustard seeds and cumin seeds and cook, shaking the pan occasionally, for 1 minute.

5 Add the garlic, ginger, curry leaves (watch out, they'll spit!) and Kashmiri chilli powder. Cook, stirring frequently, for another 1 minute, then season with salt and pepper and remove the pan from the heat.

6 To serve, spread the yoghurt on to a plate and top it with the cauliflower pieces. Spoon the tarka over the top. Serve drizzled with the spiced butter and with flatbreads to mop up the yoghurt.

60 Minutes or More

Slow cooking is my favourite kind of cooking. The recipes in this chapter take the longest, but I'd argue that they're some of the easiest to make – because even though they may not arrive at the table in speedy minutes, they're mostly about letting time do the work.

Some of the best flavours develop when you do nothing at all. In these recipes, patience, not labour, leads to something incredibly delicious. There's time to braise meats until they're fall-apart tender, caramelise onions until rich and sweet, slow-roast vegetables until perfectly jammy, and build deeply flavourful curries and stews.

Some of the most iconic recipes (even if I do say so myself) live in this chapter – like my NFC (Nigerian Fried Chicken), 'Nduja & Sausage Meatballs and my Mum's Nigerian Chicken Stew. They are, of course, among the longer cooks in the book, but I promise they are still incredibly easy. And, as the saying goes, all good things come to those who wait.

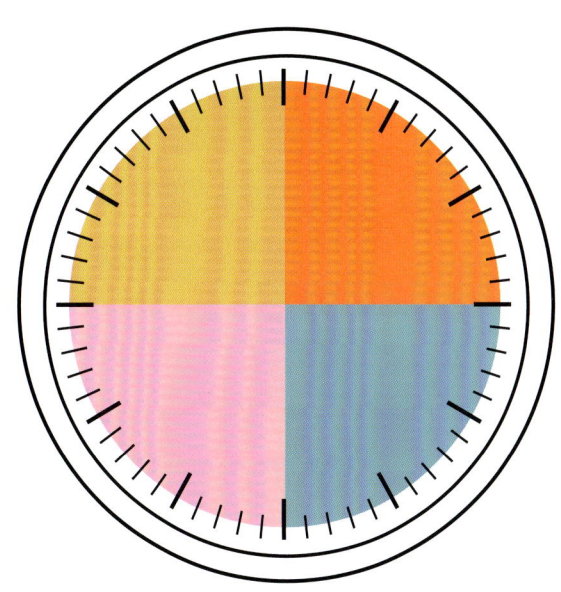

In this chapter

'Nduja & Sausage Meatballs

1 hour 15 minutes

Serves 4

2 × 400g tins of good-quality
   crushed tomatoes
2 tbsp extra-virgin olive oil,
   plus more for brushing
1 onion, halved
30g fresh basil sprigs, reserve
   some of the leaves to serve
2 tsp sugar
1 large egg
30ml whole milk
30g panko breadcrumbs
20g parmigiano
   reggiano, grated
80g 'nduja, softened at room
   temperature for 30 minutes
450g pork sausagemeat
Crusty bread or spaghetti,
   to serve

For me, a perfect meatball is juicy, well seasoned and so tender that a spoon can glide through it with ease. These meatballs deliver just that, thanks to a flavour-packed mixture of sausagemeat and 'nduja.

As making meatballs is a bit of a labour of love, I've kept the sauce simple. Inspired by Marcella Hazan's iconic tomato sauce (simmered tinned tomatoes with lots of butter – 5 tablespoons per tin – and a halved onion), this version swaps butter for extra-virgin olive oil and dials back the richness, letting the meatballs take centre stage.

Serve the onion in the sauce alongside the meatballs, if you like. Marcella Hazan discards it, but I think it's too flavourful to waste.

1   Place the tinned tomatoes, olive oil, onion, basil and sugar into a medium saucepan. Swirl 200ml of cold water around the empty tins, then tip that into the pan, too. Season with salt and pepper, stir to combine and bring the sauce to a simmer over a medium–high heat. Reduce the heat to medium–low and simmer, uncovered, for 40 minutes. I recommend setting a timer (you'll refer back to it later).

2   Meanwhile, beat the egg in a medium mixing bowl. Add the milk, panko and parmigiano reggiano and mix to form a paste. Season with black pepper (no need for salt). Add the softened 'nduja to the paste, mashing it down with the back of a spoon and folding it in until well incorporated. Add the sausagemeat and use your hands to mix until everything is thoroughly combined. Roll the mixture into 12 equally sized balls and refrigerate to firm up.

3   Heat your oven grill to high. Line a baking tray with foil and lightly brush it with olive oil.

4   When there are 15 minutes left on your timer, arrange the chilled meatballs in a single layer on the prepared tray. Brush them lightly with olive oil and grill for 7–10 minutes, or until browned on top – they won't be cooked through, but the browning brings incredible flavour.

5   Once the timer for the sauce goes off, add the browned meatballs to the pan and stir gently to combine. Cover with a lid, and simmer the meatballs in the sauce for 15 minutes. Taste the sauce and season with salt and pepper, if needed, then serve with crusty bread or piled on to spaghetti. (And don't forget the onion, if you fancy.)

Aromatic Thai Duck Noodle Soup

2 hours 30 minutes

Serves 4–6

3 × 7cm cinnamon sticks
4 star anise
2 tsp Sichuan peppercorns
1 tsp coriander seeds
1 tsp black peppercorns
4 tbsp light soy sauce
2 tbsp dark soy sauce
2 tbsp oyster sauce
2 tbsp palm sugar (or light
   brown soft sugar)
30g fresh ginger, sliced (no
   need to peel)
8 garlic cloves, smashed
4 duck legs

**For the chilli garlic
vinegar (optional)**

4 tbsp distilled white vinegar
2 garlic cloves, finely grated
   or minced
½ red chilli, finely chopped
   (deseed for less heat)

To serve
4–6 portions of noodles (fresh
   egg noodles or fresh wonton
   noodles work best)
1 small handful of fresh
   coriander, leaves and tender
   stems roughly chopped

This is one of the most delicious noodle soups you'll ever make. The broth is rich, aromatic and packed with warm spices, and the duck just melts in your mouth. Yes, the ingredient list is long, but please don't let that put you off – the method is very straightforward. Simply toast your spices to unlock their fragrance, then throw everything else into the pot and let time do all the work.

*If you have a spice bag or muslin cloth, use it to **bundle the toasted spices, ginger and garlic**, simply lifting it out at the end to save having to strain the broth – and on things to wash up!*

1 Set a large cast-iron casserole (Dutch oven) or heavy-based pan over a medium–high heat. Add the cinnamon sticks, star anise, Sichuan peppercorns, coriander seeds and black peppercorns and toast them, stirring frequently, until the coriander seeds darken slightly and the spices are nice and aromatic (around 1–2 minutes).

2 Add 2 litres of water, along with both soy sauces, and the oyster sauce, palm sugar, ginger and garlic. Turn the heat up to high, stir the liquid and bring it to a simmer. Add the duck legs, return to a simmer, then reduce the heat to low, cover the pan with a lid and cook the broth for 2 hours, or until the duck is tender and falling off the bone.

3 Meanwhile, make the chilli garlic vinegar, if using. Simply combine the ingredients in a small bowl and set aside until you're ready to serve.

4 Using tongs, transfer the duck legs to a chopping board. Let them cool for 10–15 minutes. Meanwhile, skim off any fat from the surface of the broth, then strain the broth through a sieve into a bowl. Wipe out the casserole pan (no need to wash it). Pour the broth back in.

5 Once the duck is cool enough to handle, remove and discard the skin and bones, then shred the meat. Set aside.

6 In a separate pot, boil the noodles in well-salted water according to the package instructions. Drain and divide them between your serving bowls. Top with the shredded duck meat.

7 Reheat the broth until boiling, then ladle it over the noodles and duck. Top with coriander and, if using, a teaspoon (or more, to taste) of chilli garlic vinegar for an extra kick.

Mum's Nigerian Chicken Stew

1 hour 30 minutes

Serves 6–8

1kg skin-on, bone-in chicken
   thighs (see note, page 126)
2 tbsp vegetable oil (or
   any neutral oil)
2 tsp curry powder (mild,
   medium or hot)
2 tsp dried thyme
1 tsp cayenne
   pepper (optional)

For the stew base
1 large red pepper, deseeded
   and roughly chopped
2 vine tomatoes (around 150g),
   roughly chopped
1 red onion, roughly chopped
2 red scotch bonnet chillies,
   quartered (or use 1 for
   milder heat)
25g fresh ginger, peeled and
   roughly chopped
1 tsp fine sea salt

For the stew
150ml vegetable oil (or
   any neutral oil)
1 red onion, finely chopped
150g double-concentrate
   tomato purée
1 tbsp curry powder (mild,
   medium or hot)
2 tsp dried thyme
2 dried bay leaves
1 chicken stock pot

There's no dish more nostalgic to me than Nigerian chicken stew. For a start, it's the first thing my mum taught me to cook. Every family has their way of making it – this is ours (though Mum's version was a little different).

The amount of oil this recipe calls for might surprise you, but it really is essential. Proper Nigerian stew isn't just simmered; it's fried, and that's what gives it its deep, savoury flavour. But don't worry, once the stew's done, the oil naturally pools on top, making it easy to skim off. What's left behind is tender, perfectly seasoned chicken in a thick, flavour-packed sauce that's perfect with rice, plantain, and some veg for balance.

1   Place the chicken in a large bowl with the oil, curry powder, dried thyme, cayenne pepper (if using) and a generous pinch of salt. Toss to coat, then marinate for at least 1 hour, or overnight if you can. If you're short on time, just let it sit while you prep the stew base.

2   To make the stew base, in a blender, blitz the red pepper, tomatoes, onion, chillies, ginger, sea salt and 100ml of water in a blender until smooth. Set aside.

3   On to the stew. Heat the 150ml of oil in a large cast-iron casserole (Dutch oven) over a medium–high heat. Working in batches, brown the chicken, skin-side down, for 3–5 minutes, then flip it and cook it for further 2–3 minutes. Transfer each batch to a plate, leaving the oil in the pan. The chicken won't be cooked through at this stage – it'll finish cooking in the stew.

4   Turn the heat down to medium. Add the onion to the pot and cook, stirring occasionally, until the onion has softened and is starting to brown (around 3–5 minutes).

5   Add the tomato purée and cook, stirring frequently, until it darkens (about another 3–5 minutes).

6   Pour in the blended stew base, stir to combine and bring the liquid to a simmer. Partially cover the pot with a lid (the stew will splatter!) and simmer, removing the lid to stir occasionally, until the sauce has reduced by about one third and the oil has started to pool on top (around 15 minutes).

To serve

Cooked white basmati rice (or
  your favourite rice)
Fried, baked or grilled
  ripe plantain
Salad or steamed greens

7   Stir in the curry powder, dried thyme, dried bay leaves, stock pot and 250ml of water. Season with salt and pepper, then nestle in the part-cooked chicken along with any resting juices.

8   Bring the liquid to a simmer over a medium–high heat, then reduce the heat to medium–low, cover fully with the lid, and simmer for 30 minutes, until the oil separates and the chicken is tender. By this point, the oil has done its job, so I like to skim most of it off before serving – it's easy to do because the stew is so thick and the oil just pools on top.

9   Serve the stew with steamed rice and fried plantain (plus some veg for health!) for a quintessential Nigerian dinner.

One-Pan Crispy Roast Chicken with Lemon Garlic Potatoes

1 hour, plus overnight dry-brining

Serves 4–6

1 medium whole chicken
  (around 1.6kg)
1kg Maris Piper potatoes,
  peeled and cut into 1.5cm
  slices (choose similar-sized
  potatoes for even cooking)
75g butter, melted (or extra-
  virgin olive oil, for dairy-free)
1 lemon, zest and juice
4 garlic cloves, finely grated
  or minced
1 tsp fine sea salt, plus more
  for dry brining
200ml chicken stock
1 tbsp vegetable or extra-virgin
  olive oil

I firmly believe that the best roast chicken needs only one ingredient: salt. Plus one non-ingredient: time. Dry brining – aka salting the chicken and refrigerating overnight – does three key things. First, it seasons the meat through to the bone. Second, it keeps it nice and juicy, even the breast! Third, it dries out the skin, which helps it brown and crisp up beautifully. Here, the chicken is roasted on top of lemony, garlicky, buttery potatoes, which absorb the delicious chicken juices. It makes for a truly stellar Sunday roast.

*This is a great recipe to **use up any herbs** that are wilting in the fridge. Hard, woody herbs like rosemary and thyme can go in with the potatoes before roasting, while finely chopped soft herbs like parsley and chives can be stirred through just before serving.*

1 Start by spatchcocking your chicken – it's easier than you think (or ask your butcher to do it). Place it on a chopping board, breast-side down, cavity facing you. Using sharp scissors, cut down each side of the backbone and remove it (save it for stock). Open out the chicken, flip it over and press down on the breastbone to flatten.

2 Season the chicken with salt on both sides, then transfer it to a wire rack set in a large roasting tin. Leave it uncovered in the fridge overnight, or up to 24 hours. Dry brining is non-negotiable here, but if you're short on time, let it sit in the fridge for at least 1 hour. Take the chicken out of the fridge 30 minutes to 1 hour before cooking so that it comes to room temperature. Heat your oven to 220°C/200°C fan.

3 In a large roasting tin, toss the potatoes with the butter, lemon zest and juice, garlic and teaspoon of salt. Spread them out in a single layer, then pour in the chicken stock.

4 Pat the chicken dry with kitchen paper. Place it on top of the potatoes skin-side up, then rub it with the oil. Roast for 35–40 minutes, or until the chicken reaches an internal temperature of 75°C. Alternatively, pierce the chicken between the leg and the body or at the thickest part of the breast – the juices should run clear.

5 Rest the chicken, covered, for 10–15 minutes to let the juices settle, then carve. Serve with the potatoes, spooning over the juices.

Oven-Baked Jollof Rice

2 hours

Serves 8

600g long-grain rice (I use
   Ben's Original)
150ml vegetable oil
1 onion, finely chopped
60g double-concentrate
   tomato purée
1 tbsp curry powder (mild,
   medium or hot)
1 tbsp dried thyme
3 chicken or vegetable
   stock cubes
2 dried bay leaves
600ml boiling water
Grilled chicken and fried
   plantain, to serve (optional)

For the stew base

4 vine tomatoes (around
   300g), halved and deseeded
1 red pepper, deseeded and
   cut into large chunks
1 onion, cut into large chunks
1 red scotch bonnet chilli,
   stem removed
1 tbsp vegetable oil (or any
   neutral oil)
15g fresh ginger, peeled and
   roughly chopped
1 tsp fine sea salt

Jollof rice has deep roots in West African culture – and call me biased, but I think Nigerian jollof reigns supreme. It is essentially rice cooked in a spicy, flavour-packed tomato sauce, which sounds simple, but is actually pretty difficult to nail. From burning the base and ending up with bitter rice, to going too far the other way and making jollof risotto (which nobody wants), much can go wrong.

Switching to oven-baking my jollof rice single handedly changed the game for me. It's by no means traditional, but it's the most foolproof method I've found for nailing it every single time. It's one of the most popular recipes on my socials and blog for exactly that reason.

*I generally use two **scotch bonnets**, which makes what I would call a spicy jollof rice. For a mild version, use half a scotch bonnet instead. For a medium jollof rice, use one. For a blow-your-head-off spicy jollof rice, use three or more (at your own risk!).*

1 Start with the stew base. Heat your oven to 220°C/200°C fan.

2 Place the tomatoes, red pepper, onion and chilli in a medium roasting tin. Drizzle over the vegetable oil and toss to coat. Roast the vegetables for 25–30 minutes, or until they are softened and charred at the edges. Remove from the oven and leave to cool for 10 minutes. Turn the oven down to 180°C/160°C fan.

3 While the vegetables are roasting and cooling, thoroughly wash the long-grain rice with cold water until the water runs clear, then drain. Please don't rush this step. The goal is to remove as much of the starch as possible, which is what is going to give you separate, non-sticky cooked grains of jollof rice. Leave the rice to drain in a sieve until you need it.

4 Transfer the cooled roasted vegetables to a blender. Add the ginger and salt and blitz until smooth. Set aside.

5 Heat the 150ml of oil in a large cast-iron casserole (Dutch oven) set over a medium heat (you can use a large saucepan if you don't have a cast-iron casserole). Add the onion and cook, stirring occasionally, until softened and beginning to brown (around 6–8 minutes). Add the tomato purée and cook, stirring frequently, until it begins to darken (3–5 minutes).

6 Add the blended stew base to the pot, stir to combine, then partially cover the pot with a lid and bring the base to a simmer. Cook, stirring occasionally, until the oil separates from the stew (around 5 minutes).

7 Add the curry powder and dried thyme and cook, stirring almost constantly for 1 minute, then add the stock cubes, dried bay leaves and boiling water. Whisk well to dissolve the stock cubes.

8 Tip the washed and drained rice into the pot and stir to combine. Taste the liquid, then adjust the salt level to your liking – the liquid should be well seasoned. Once the rice begins to gurgle, cover the pot with the lid again and transfer it to the oven. Bake the rice mixture for 50 minutes. (If you don't have a cast-iron casserole, transfer the contents of the pot to a large, deep roasting tin. Add an extra 50ml of boiling water, cover very tightly with three layers of foil and bake for 50 minutes.)

9 Remove the pot from the oven and leave it covered for 15 minutes – the steam inside will finish cooking the rice.

10 Once the 15 minutes are up, remove the bay leaves, give the rice a stir and you're ready to serve, preferably with grilled chicken and fried plantain.

NFC (Nigerian Fried Chicken)

1 hour 15 minutes, plus overnight dry brining

Serves 4–6

2 tsp curry powder (mild, medium or hot)
2 tsp dried thyme
2 tsp onion granules or powder
1 tsp smoked paprika
1 tsp cayenne pepper (optional)
1½ tsp fine sea salt
1kg skinless, bone-in chicken thighs and/or drumsticks
Vegetable oil (or any neutral oil), for deep-frying

For the breading and frying
400g '00' flour (plain flour works, too)
2 tsp dried thyme
2 tsp curry powder (mild, medium or hot)
2 tsp onion granules or powder
1 tsp smoked paprika
1 tsp fine sea salt
½ tsp cayenne pepper (optional)
2 large eggs
240ml whole milk

For the scotch bonnet honey (optional)
120g runny honey
1 red scotch bonnet chilli, thinly sliced

This is fried chicken, but not as you know it. Inspired by my Nigerian roots, it's packed with warm, earthy spices and, honestly, it's some of the best fried chicken I've ever had – hopefully, it'll be some of the best you've ever had, too! Rather than dealing with the fuss and mess of a traditional wet brine, I've opted for a simple dry one. This ensures deeply flavoured, juicy chicken. Using ultra-fine Italian '00' flour creates an exceptionally crunchy coating that stays crisp long after frying. Frying the chicken at a slightly lower temperature gently cooks the meat, locking in juiciness, while giving the crust enough time to become super crunchy. Finished with a drizzle of scotch bonnet honey to offset all that savouriness, this is truly elite fried chicken, if I do say so myself.

*You can **adjust the heat level of the scotch bonnet honey** by how you prepare the chilli – the more you break it down, the spicier the result will be (and you can remove the seeds for less heat, too):*

- *Whole poked with a couple of small holes: mild*

- *Halved: medium-hot*

- *Thinly sliced: hot*

- *Finely minced: very hot.*

1 In a large bowl, whisk together the curry powder, dried thyme, onion granules or powder, smoked paprika, cayenne pepper (if using) and salt until well combined. Add the chicken pieces and toss well to coat, ensuring they are all evenly seasoned.

2 Arrange the seasoned chicken on a wire rack set over a baking tray. Refrigerate, uncovered, overnight, or for up to 24 hours. Remove the chicken from the fridge 30 minutes before frying.

3 Fill a large, deep cast-iron casserole (Dutch oven) halfway with vegetable oil. Heat over a medium–high heat until the temperature of the oil reaches 160°C on a cooking thermometer (I highly recommend using a thermometer for this one – I haven't found a reliable non-thermometer method for 160°C). Finally, place a clean wire rack over a large baking tray – this is where you'll transfer the cooked chicken.

continued overleaf . . .

4 While the oil is coming to temperature, in a large bowl, combine the flour, dried thyme, curry powder, onion granules or powder, smoked paprika, salt and cayenne pepper (if using) until well-combined – this is your dry mix. In a separate bowl, whisk together the eggs and milk until fully combined – this is your wet mix.

5 Drizzle 3 tablespoons of the wet mix into the dry mix and gently toss to combine – this is what creates those delicious crispy, craggy bits.

6 Working with one piece of chicken at a time, use your 'dry' hand to coat the chicken in the dry mix, ensuring it's fully covered. Shake off any excess, then use your 'wet' hand to dip it into the wet mix. Allow the excess to drip off, then return the chicken to the dry mix and use your 'dry' hand to dredge it, ensuring it's evenly coated with lots of craggy bits. Set the coated piece aside on a plate and repeat with the remaining chicken.

7 Working in batches, fry the chicken for 16 minutes per batch, flipping once halfway through, or until the coating is golden and the chicken is cooked through. Transfer the cooked pieces to the wire rack to drain. (Draining the chicken on a rack allows the air to circulate around it, keeping it nice and crispy.) You can keep it warm in a low oven while you fry the rest of the chicken.

8 If you're making the scotch bonnet honey, place the honey and scotch bonnet in a small saucepan set over a medium heat. Bring the honey to a simmer, then remove the pan from the heat. Drizzle the honey over the chicken just before serving.

Slow-Roasted Citrus Salmon

1 hour

Serves 4–6

1 side of salmon (1–1.2kg)
2 tbsp za'atar, plus more for
   finishing
2 large garlic cloves, finely
   grated or minced
Extra-virgin olive oil
1 orange, thinly sliced to
   4mm thick
1 lemon, thinly sliced to
   4mm thick

Outrageously tender and effortlessly impressive, this salmon is a true showstopper. Roasting the salmon at such a low temperature gives it the most incredible texture – soft and moist while becoming perfectly cooked all the way through. The citrus and za'atar bring balance and bold flavour. Best of all, this dish is as much a feast for the eyes as it is for the palate.

1   Heat your oven to 110°C/90°C fan. Line a large baking tray with baking paper and place the salmon on top.

2   Sprinkle the salmon with the 2 tablespoons of za'atar, add the garlic and season well with salt and pepper. Drizzle generously with extra-virgin olive oil, then rub the seasoning all over the salmon, ensuring it's evenly coated.

3   Layer the orange and lemon slices over the top of the salmon, then add a final drizzle of extra-virgin olive oil.

4   Roast the salmon for 40–50 minutes, or until the thickest part of the fillet just begins to flake when gently prodded with a knife or your finger.

5   Leave the fish to cool slightly, then carefully lift it on to a serving platter. Sprinkle with a bit more za'atar, and serve.

Slow-Cooked Massaman Lamb Shoulder

6 hours

Serves 6–8

1 bone-in lamb shoulder
(2–2.5kg), fat trimmed (ask
your butcher to help you
with this)
115g good-quality massaman
curry paste (Mae Ploy and
Thai Taste are my favourites)
2 × 400g tins of good-quality
coconut milk (at least 70%
coconut extract)
400ml chicken stock
2 tbsp light or dark brown
soft sugar
2 tbsp fish sauce
2 × 7cm cinnamon sticks
2 star anise
Cooked jasmine rice and
green vegetables, to serve

To garnish
30g roasted peanuts,
roughly chopped
1 small handful of fresh
coriander, leaves and tender
stems finely chopped
1 red chilli, thinly
sliced (optional)

This is slow-cooking at its best. The lamb becomes meltingly tender, soaking up the rich, aromatic flavours of the massaman curry, coconut milk and warm spices. Finished with crunchy peanuts and fresh coriander, it's indulgent but approachable – perfect for an impressive yet comforting meal.

Massaman curry paste is widely available in Southeast Asian supermarkets and many pan-Asian stores. If you don't have one nearby, the paste is easily found online, and it keeps for ages so don't worry about it going to waste.

1 Heat your oven to 220°C/200°C fan. Lightly season the lamb shoulder with salt on both sides.

2 Add the massaman curry paste, coconut milk, chicken stock, sugar and fish sauce to a large, deep roasting tin and roast for 10 minutes to warm the ingredients through (it makes it easier to mix). Remove the tin from the oven and whisk the paste mixture until fully combined, then add the cinnamon sticks and star anise.

3 Add the lamb, turning it to coat in the sauce, then position it fat-side down. Tightly cover the tin with a double layer of foil, then roast for 30 minutes before lowering the oven temperature to 150°C/130°C fan.

4 Continue roasting for around 5 hours, or until the lamb is almost fall-apart tender. You can start checking it at the 4-hour mark.

5 Take the tin out of the oven and increase the heat to 220°C/200°C fan. Remove the foil and carefully flip the lamb meat-side up. Baste with the sauce and roast uncovered for 25–30 minutes or until browned.

6 Transfer the lamb to a large platter and let it rest for 15–20 minutes, loosely covered with foil. Meanwhile, skim most of the excess fat from the surface of the sauce (leave the fat to cool before discarding).

7 To serve, discard the lamb bones and shred the meat with two forks. Place it on a large platter, pour over plenty of the sauce and transfer the remaining sauce to a gravy boat to serve alongside. Top with the crushed peanuts, coriander and chilli (if using). I like to serve it with steamed rice and some green vegetables.

Saucy Pork Adobo

1 hour and 35 minutes, plus 1 hour marinating

Serves 4–6

1kg pork shoulder, cut into 4cm chunks (or pork belly for a richer, fattier option)
100ml dark soy sauce
100ml vinegar (coconut, white distilled, white wine or apple cider vinegar)
8 garlic cloves, finely grated or minced
2 tbsp light or dark brown soft sugar
2 tsp coarsely ground black pepper
4 dried bay leaves
3 tbsp cornflour, mixed with 6 tbsp water
Cooked white basmati rice (or your favourite rice) and a crisp cucumber salad or slaw and pickled red onions, to serve

Some dishes just stick with you. For me, adobo is one of them. It's a cornerstone of Filipino cooking, where meat is braised in soy sauce, vinegar and aromatics until it's meltingly tender. My nanny, Janet, used to make it all the time, and no matter how many versions I try, it's hers that I always come back to.

This is my take on her recipe. It's delightfully simple – you throw everything into a pot, let it marinate, then braise until the pork is beautifully tender. I like my adobo saucier than usual, with plenty of thickened gravy to pour over hot rice. It truly is the epitome of comfort food. Just one thing, though: don't swap dark soy for light soy – it's much saltier and will throw off the balance.

1   Place the pork, soy sauce, vinegar, garlic, sugar, black pepper and bay leaves in a medium saucepan. Toss to coat the pork, then transfer the pan to the fridge and marinate the meat for 1 hour.

2   Stir in 1 litre of cold water and bring it to a gentle simmer over a medium–high heat. Lower the heat to medium and skim off the foam that rises to the surface. Cover the pan with a lid, reduce the heat to low or medium–low and simmer for 1 hour 30 minutes, or until the pork is beautifully tender.

3   Turn the heat up to medium–high, add the cornflour slurry and cook for 1–2 minutes, or until the sauce thickens slightly.

4   Serve with steamed rice and something crisp on the side – cucumber, pickled onions or a simple, zingy slaw.

Gochujang Braised Short Ribs

6 hours

Serves 6

2kg beef short ribs

1 tbsp vegetable oil (or any neutral oil)

8 garlic cloves, finely grated or minced

20g fresh ginger, finely grated or minced

100g gochujang

100ml mirin

2 tbsp dark soy sauce

2 tbsp light brown soft sugar

2 × 7cm cinnamon sticks

1–2 tbsp cornflour, mixed with 2–4 tbsp water (depending on how thick you want your sauce)

2 spring onions, very thinly sliced, to garnish

Toasted white sesame seeds, to garnish

Short ribs were made for slow braises, and this one delivers big flavours with minimal effort. After a good sear, the ribs simmer in a warm gochujang-based broth, which reduces down to a rich, glossy sauce that begs to be poured over rice or mashed potatoes.

*This is **a great dish for when you have guests**. You can make it a day in advance (up to Step 5) and the flavours will deepen overnight. To reheat, place the short ribs and sauce in a covered baking dish and warm them in a 160°C/140°C fan oven for around 30 minutes, or until heated through. Continue with Step 5, adding a splash of water to loosen, if needed, then thicken with the slurry.*

1 Heat your oven to 150°C/130°C fan. Pat the short ribs dry and season them generously with salt.

2 Heat the oil in a large cast-iron casserole (Dutch oven) over a medium–high heat. Working in batches, sear the short ribs until deeply browned on all sides (10 minutes-ish per batch – this is key for flavour, so take your time). Transfer the ribs to a plate. (If you don't have a casserole, sear the ribs in batches in a large pan, then transfer them to a deep, ovenproof dish in a single layer. Continue with Step 3 in the used pan, but then pour the sauce over the ribs in the dish before covering with a double layer of foil to bake.)

3 Lower the heat to medium. Add the garlic and ginger, and cook, stirring to prevent burning, for 30 seconds. Pour in 1 litre of water, then add the gochujang, mirin, soy sauce, sugar and cinnamon sticks. Stir, then turn the heat back up to medium–high and bring to a simmer, scraping up any browned bits from the bottom of the pot.

4 Return the short ribs (along with any juices) to the pot, bone-side up, and bring everything back to a simmer. Cover with a lid and bake for 4–5 hours, or until the meat is falling off the bone.

5 Transfer the short ribs to a large plate or chopping board and let them rest for 10 minutes. Meanwhile, skim off the excess fat from the surface of the sauce. Transfer the sauce to a saucepan, stir in the cornflour slurry and cook, stirring, until thickened (2–3 minutes). Spoon the sauce over the short ribs and finish with the spring onions and a sprinkle of toasted sesame seeds.

Spiced Red Lentil Dal

Inspired by *masoor dal tadka*, this is a wonderfully creamy red lentil dish finished with spiced ghee. It's comforting, full of flavour and incredibly easy to make. Simply cook the lentils until soft and creamy, then bloom some aromatics and spices in hot ghee. Bring the two together and you've got the perfect bowl.

Food writer and best-selling author Priya Krishna describes **asafoetida** *(hing in Hindi) as an ingredient that 'makes Indian food taste more Indian'. Flavour-wise, it's funky, oniony and garlicky – but more importantly, it's a flavour enhancer, making every other spice come through. You can find it in most large UK supermarkets.*

1 hour

Serves 4

200g red split lentils
2 vine tomatoes (about 150g), finely chopped
1 small onion, finely chopped
1 green chilli, finely chopped (deseeded for less heat)
¾ tsp fine sea salt
½ tsp ground turmeric
Pinch of asafoetida (hing)
Cooked white basmati rice or warmed naan breads, to serve

For the tadka
3 tbsp ghee
½ tbsp cumin seeds
1 tsp black mustard seeds (or 1½ tsp yellow mustard seeds, if you can't find the black variety)
2 garlic cloves, finely grated or minced
10g fresh ginger, finely grated or minced
Big pinch of asafoetida (hing)
¼ tsp mild Kashmiri chilli powder
¼ tsp garam masala

1 Rinse the lentils under cold water until the water runs clear, then drain. Tip the lentils into a large saucepan with the tomatoes, onion, chilli, salt, turmeric, asafoetida and 850ml of water. Stir to combine and bring the water to a simmer over a high heat.

2 Skim off any froth or foam that rises to the top, then cover the pan with a lid, reduce the heat to low and cook the lentils, stirring occasionally, for 45 minutes, or until they are soft and have broken down to a creamy consistency.

3 When the lentils are nearly done, make the tadka. Heat the ghee in a small saucepan over a medium–low heat. Add the cumin and mustard seeds and cook for 1 minute, stirring frequently.

4 Add the garlic and ginger and cook for another 1 minute, stirring constantly. Finally, stir in the asafoetida, Kashmiri chilli powder and garam masala. Cook for 30 seconds – these spices burn easily, so keep a close eye.

5 Pour the tadka into the dal and stir through. Taste and adjust the salt level to your liking, then serve with rice or naan.

Charred Spring Onion, Chicken & Orzo Soup

1 hour

Serves 4–6

1 bunch of spring onions (around 100g), trimmed, plus optional extra thinly sliced to garnish

2 litres chicken stock

50g fresh ginger, cut into 5mm slices (no need to peel)

1 onion, quartered (no need to peel)

1 large carrot, roughly chopped

1 whole garlic bulb, halved horizontally (no need to peel)

2 tbsp fish sauce (or light soy sauce)

2 tbsp Shaoxing wine

1 tsp ground turmeric

½ tsp fine sea salt

4 skin-on, bone-in chicken thighs (see note, page 126)

225g dried orzo

250g pak choi, sliced into 2cm pieces

Chilli oil, for drizzling (optional)

This soup is my answer to grey London days when all I want is something warm and nourishing. It's a perfect example of how small, thoughtful steps can unlock big flavours. Charring the spring onions right at the start adds a smoky depth and subtle sweetness to the broth. From there, it becomes a throw-everything-into-the-pot type of recipe – the best kind, really. If you're anything like me, it'll be one you turn to time and again when you just need a bit of comfort.

1 Set a large cast-iron casserole (Dutch oven) or heavy-based pot over a medium–high heat. Add the spring onions and cook for around 1 minute per side, until deeply charred.

2 Pour in the chicken stock, scraping up any browned bits from the base of the pot. Add the ginger, onion, carrot, garlic, fish sauce (or soy sauce), Shaoxing wine, turmeric and salt and stir to combine. Add the chicken thighs and bring everything to a simmer.

3 Skim off any foam that rises to the surface, then turn the heat down to medium–low, cover with a lid and simmer for 30 minutes, or until the chicken is fall-apart tender.

4 Lift out the chicken and set it aside until cool enough to handle, then discard the skin and bones and shred the meat.

5 Strain the broth into a clean pot, pressing down on the solids to extract every bit of flavour. Taste and adjust the salt level – you might find it doesn't need anything more. Bring the broth back to the boil over a medium–high heat.

6 Rinse the orzo under cold water to wash away the excess starch, then stir the pasta into the broth. Simmer for about 9 minutes, or until the pasta is just shy of al dente.

7 Add the shredded chicken and pak choi, letting everything simmer for another minute or two, or until the pak choi is wilted but still vibrant.

8 Ladle the soup into bowls, top with extra sliced spring onion, as well as a drizzle of chilli oil if you wish, then serve.

'Nduja Confit Tomatoes with Whipped Ricotta

1 hour

Serves 4

75ml extra-virgin olive oil
80g 'nduja
500g sweet, ripe
  cherry tomatoes
6 garlic cloves, peeled
1 tsp sugar
1 small handful of fresh basil
  leaves, half thinly sliced,
  half left whole (small ones
  if possible)
250g ricotta
Crusty bread, or pasta,
  to serve

I love slow-roasting cherry tomatoes. They soften, burst and slowly collapse into a thick, sticky sauce that's sweet, sharp and savoury all at once. Here, we take things a step further by confiting them – cooking them low and slow in plenty of olive oil spiked with 'nduja, which brings heat, depth and a little funk (the good kind!). I like to pile the whole thing over whipped ricotta and serve it with crusty bread, but it's just as – if not more – delicious stirred through pasta.

1   Heat your oven to 180°C/160°C fan.

2   Add the olive oil and 'nduja to a cold, large frying pan or sauté pan – ideally one that's ovenproof, but if not, you can transfer the tomato mixture to a roasting dish later.

3   Set the pan over a medium heat. As it warms, the 'nduja will start to melt. Use a wooden spoon to break it up and stir it into the oil to create a punchy red paste.

4   Add the cherry tomatoes, garlic and sugar. Season with salt and pepper, then toss everything together so the tomatoes are well coated in the spicy oil. If your pan isn't ovenproof, tip it all into a roasting dish. Roast for 35–45 minutes, or until the tomatoes are blistered, juicy and bubbling. Stir through the sliced basil and leave it all to cool slightly.

5   In a bowl, whisk the ricotta until smooth, then season with a little salt and whisk again. Spread the ricotta on to a serving plate, then spoon the confit tomatoes and garlicky 'nduja oil over the top. Finish with whole basil leaves and serve with crusty bread for mopping, or stirred through your favourite pasta for something more substantial.

Fragrant Lamb & Spinach Curry

2 hours 40 minutes

Serves 6

1kg diced lamb
4 tbsp vegetable oil or
 coconut oil
4 × 7cm cinnamon sticks
1 star anise
½ tsp cumin seeds
2 large onions, thinly sliced
2 tbsp garlic and ginger paste
 (or 1 tbsp each of garlic paste
 and ginger paste)
1 tbsp mild Kashmiri
 chilli powder
1 tsp ground cumin
1 tsp ground coriander
1 tsp ground turmeric
1 × 400g tin of good-quality
 crushed tomatoes
1 × 400g tin of good-quality
 coconut milk (70% or more
 coconut extract)
2 chicken stock cubes
2 dried bay leaves
200g baby spinach
30g fresh coriander,
 leaves and tender stems
 roughly chopped
1 small handful of flaked
 almonds, to garnish
Cooked white basmati rice
 and/or warmed flatbreads,
 to serve

The best curries don't need to be complicated, but they do need time – and this one is worth every minute. It starts with cinnamon and cumin sizzling in hot oil. Next come the onions, slow-cooked until sweet, before warm spices, tinned tomatoes and coconut milk join the mix. The lamb then gently simmers in the fragrant sauce until fall-apart-tender, ready to be scooped up with rice or folded into soft, fluffy flatbreads. The last-minute addition of spinach and coriander keeps things bright – because even slow-cooked comfort food needs just a little freshness.

*For this dish, I'm a fan of **lamb from the butcher** rather than the supermarket, but don't worry if that's all that's available – the lamb will be a little leaner, and therefore drier, but just as delicious.*

1 Season the lamb with salt and pepper, toss to coat the cubes in the seasoning and set aside to come to room temperature.

2 Heat the oil in a large cast-iron casserole (Dutch oven) over a medium heat. Add the cinnamon sticks, star anise and cumin seeds and cook, shaking the pan occasionally, for 1–2 minutes.

3 Add the onions with a good pinch of salt and cook, stirring occasionally, for 20 minutes, or until softened and beginning to brown.

4 Stir in the ginger and garlic paste, chilli powder, ground cumin, ground coriander and ground turmeric. Cook, stirring frequently for 1 minute, then add the lamb, tinned tomatoes, coconut milk, stock cubes and dried bay leaves. Season with salt and pepper, stir to combine and bring the liquid to a simmer over a medium–high heat.

5 Once simmering, cover the pot, reduce the heat to low or medium–low and cook for 1½–2 hours, or until the lamb is nice and tender.

6 Taste, and adjust the salt level to your liking, then stir through the baby spinach. Reserve a little of the fresh coriander for garnish, then stir through the remainder. Serve topped with the reserved coriander and flaked almonds, alongside steamed rice and/or warmed flatbreads.

Smoky Harissa Mushroom Ragù

1 hour 15 minutes

Serves 4

300g oyster mushrooms, torn
    into 5mm-ish strips
3 tbsp extra virgin olive oil
½ tsp smoked paprika
1 large onion, finely chopped
4 garlic cloves, finely grated
    or minced
2 tbsp double-concentrate
    tomato purée
2 tbsp harissa paste
100ml white wine
1 × 400g tin of good-quality
    crushed tomatoes
1 tbsp light soy sauce
1 tsp sugar
1 small handful of fresh flat-leaf
    parsley, leaves and tender
    stems roughly chopped,
    to serve
Pasta, mashed potato or
    cheesy polenta, to serve

This is a bold claim, but I genuinely believe that this mushroom ragù has the power to convert both the most avid of meat eaters *and* self-proclaimed mushroom haters. It's deeply savoury, packed with flavour and surprisingly meaty for something that's entirely plant-based.

Dry-sautéing the mushrooms is key – you're essentially extracting the excess moisture, which intensifies their umaminess and gives them a lovely char. The harissa brings complexity and a smidge of heat, while a touch of paprika adds smokiness. This ragù is, of course, fantastic with pasta, but also works really nicely served over mashed potatoes or cheesy polenta.

1   Set a large heavy-based sauté pan or cast-iron casserole (Dutch oven) over a high heat. Once hot, add the mushrooms without any oil and dry sauté, stirring now and then, for 6 minutes, or until they release their moisture and the pan is dry.

2   Add 1 tablespoon of the olive oil and cook, stirring occasionally, until the mushrooms have browned (around 4 minutes). Season with salt and pepper, add the smoked paprika and cook for 30 seconds, then transfer the mushrooms to a plate.

3   Reduce the heat to medium and add the remaining 2 tablespoons of oil, followed by the onion and a generous pinch of salt. Cook, stirring occasionally, for 12–15 minutes, or until softened and golden.

4   Add the garlic and cook, stirring frequently, for 1 minute, then add the tomato purée and harissa paste and cook, stirring often, for 2–3 minutes, or until slightly darkened.

5   Pour in the white wine and let it almost completely evaporate, then add the tinned tomatoes, soy sauce, sugar and 400ml of water (simply fill the empty tomato tin with water, give it a swirl, and add that).

6   Season the sauce with salt and pepper, add the mushrooms back to the pan, and bring the liquid to a simmer, then reduce the heat to medium or medium–low and simmer, uncovered, stirring occasionally, for 45 minutes, or until thickened. Taste, and adjust the salt level to your liking, then remove the pan from the heat and stir through the parsley. Serve with your favourite pasta (or mash or polenta).

Sticky Pork Belly Bánh Mì

2 hours

Makes 2 big sandwiches

500g pork belly slices
4 tbsp hoisin sauce
1 tbsp light soy sauce
1 tbsp runny honey
1 garlic clove, finely grated
  or minced

For the pickled vegetables
150g carrot, cut into thin
  matchsticks (no need to peel)
150g daikon, cut into
  thin matchsticks
50g sugar
1 tsp fine sea salt
120ml rice vinegar
1 red chilli, halved (optional;
  deseed for less heat)

To assemble
1 crusty baguette
60g pork or chicken pâté
50g Kewpie mayonnaise (or
  regular mayo, if unavailable)
1 cucumber, thinly sliced
1 large handful of fresh
  coriander, leaves and tender
  stems roughly chopped
1 handful of crispy
  shallots (optional)

Bánh mì is truly a sensational sandwich. It's bold, bright and never boring, bringing together French and Vietnamese influences in one incredible bite. This version features succulent pork belly, glazed in a hoisin honey sauce and roasted until tender and caramelised at the edges. Paired with pickled veg, cucumber, coriander and pâté, it's the perfect balance of textures and flavours.

Kewpie is a Japanese mayonnaise made with egg yolks, which gives it a richer, more savoury flavour than regular mayo. It's slightly sweet, with a deep umami note that makes it especially good in slaws, dressings and sandwiches, or drizzled over rice bowls.

1 Heat your oven to 160°C/fan 140°C. Pat the pork belly slices dry with kitchen paper.

2 In a large bowl, combine the hoisin sauce, soy sauce, honey and garlic, then add the pork belly slices and toss to coat. Transfer the pork and any remaining sauce to a small roasting tin. Cover tightly with foil and roast for 1 hour 30 minutes, or until beautifully tender.

3 Meanwhile, prepare the pickled vegetables: place the carrot, daikon, sugar and salt in a large bowl. Massage the sugar and salt into the vegetables until dissolved, then stir in the rice vinegar, 120ml of cold water and the red chilli (if using). Cover the bowl and refrigerate the vegetables for at least 1 hour 30 minutes, while the pork is cooking (Ideally, you'd pickle them overnight; or even make them in advance and store them in a jar in the fridge for up to 1 week.)

4 Back to the pork. Once it's tender, remove the foil and switch your oven to its highest grill setting. Grill the pork slices for 3–4 minutes, turning halfway and basting with the sauce, or until they're sticky, charred and caramelised.

5 Split your baguette in half lengthways and scoop out some of the soft bread from the inside (chef's treat!). Spread the pâté along the base, then spread the mayo on top. Layer on the cucumber slices, followed by a generous helping of the (drained) pickled vegetables. Top with the pork belly, scatter over the coriander and finish with crispy shallots (if using). Sandwich with the top half of bread and slice the baguette into two across its middle. Serve immediately.

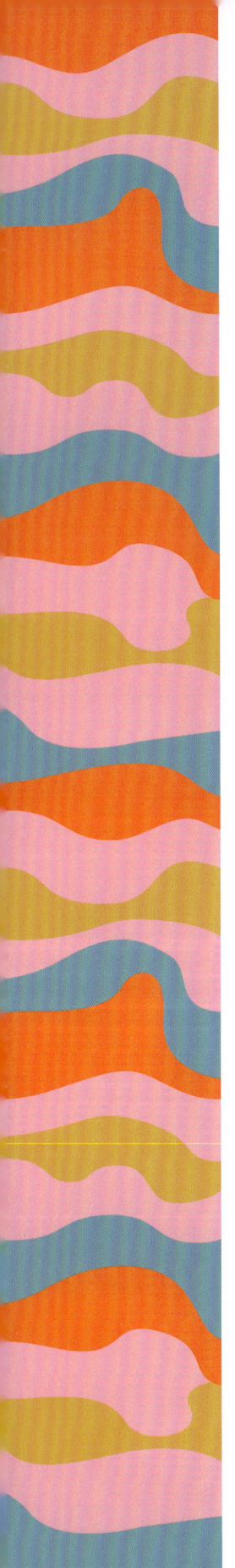

Sweet Treats

I love a good dessert (who doesn't?!) and my big flavour/deeply delicious ethos applies to them too.

This chapter is full of, dare I say, some of the most delicious puddings, bakes and treats you'll ever make. Some are quick wins, like the Caramelised Croissants with Coffee Cream – they're unbelievably good and take just 15 minutes. Others take a little longer but are well worth the time investment, like the Chai-Spiced Apple Crumble, which is golden, deeply spiced and, if I'm honest, my favourite crumble of all time. All the recipes aim for the same thing: maximum flavour, minimal faff. So, whether you're after a speedy sweet fix or a slow weekend bake, there's something here for you.

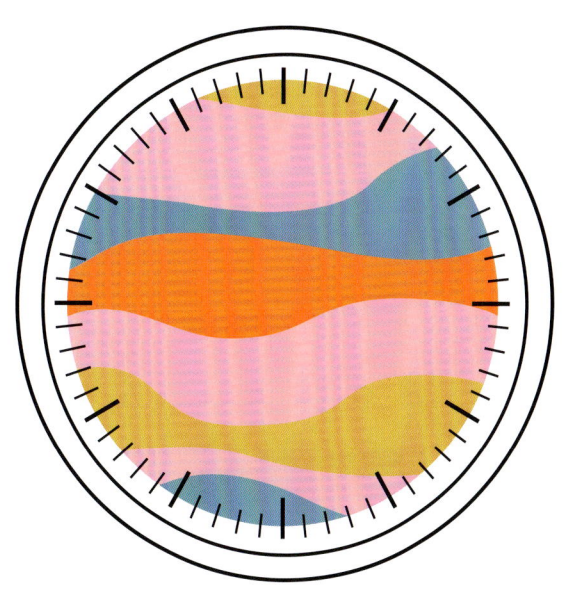

In this chapter

Strawberry & Elderflower Eton Mess

Serves 4–6

500g strawberries, hulled
1–2 tbsp elderflower cordial, to
   taste (a thicker, syrupy cordial
   works best)
450ml double cream
1–2 tbsp icing sugar, to taste
½ tsp vanilla paste (optional)
4 ready-made meringue nests

Few things capture British summertime quite like Eton Mess. This one comes with a gentle twist. I've taken the familiar trio of strawberries, meringue and cream and added just a splash of elderflower cordial, which gives the whole thing a subtle, floral lift. You don't need much, but do make sure you use a good-quality, syrupy one – some cordials are quite watery and won't deliver much flavour.

1 Blitz a third of the strawberries with the elderflower cordial until smooth. Halve or quarter the rest into bite-sized pieces.

2 Using a stand mixer fitted with the whisk, whip the double cream with the icing sugar, and the vanilla (if using) on medium speed (alternatively, use a large bowl and an electric hand mixer). Stop once the cream mixture forms soft peaks – it should just hold its shape.

3 Crumble three of the meringues into the whipped cream and add the chopped strawberries. Fold everything together gently, then add the strawberry and elderflower purée and stir briefly to ripple it through.

4 Divide the mess between six bowls or glasses and crush the final meringue over the top. Serve immediately.

Caramelised Croissants with Coffee Cream

Serves 2 very hungry people or 4 people after a big meal

2 tbsp salted butter, softened
2 tbsp light brown soft sugar
2 day-old all-butter croissants (or good-quality packaged croissants)
125g mascarpone
75ml double cream
1 tbsp icing sugar
1 tsp espresso powder or finely ground instant coffee
Toasted flaked almonds or chopped roasted hazelnuts, to serve (optional)

There's a time and a place for a perfect, buttery, bakery-fresh croissant – and this isn't it. This recipe is for the croissants you forgot about, or better yet, the shelf-stable ones you find in supermarkets. Flattened, buttered and caramelised in a pan, they turn into the most delicious, crisp, sugar-shelled pastries.

All that sweetness needs something to balance it and the coffee mascarpone cream does exactly that – it's rich, cool and just bitter enough to round things out. Add a handful of toasted nuts for crunch and you've got a stunning dessert that comes together in less than 15 minutes.

1   In a small bowl, mix the butter and brown sugar to a smooth paste.

2   Using a rolling pin (or a wine bottle!), gently flatten the croissants to about 5mm thick. Spread half of the butter mixture over one side of each croissant.

3   Heat a large non-stick frying pan over a medium heat. Place the croissants butter-side down in a single layer. Cover them with a sheet of baking paper and weigh them down with a heavy pan or something similar. Cook for 2 minutes.

4   Remove the paper, spread the remaining butter mixture over the top of the croissants, then flip. Cover again with the baking paper, weigh down with something heavy again and cook for another 2 minutes. Transfer to a clean piece of baking paper to cool slightly.

5   Meanwhile, in a small bowl, whisk together the mascarpone, double cream, icing sugar and espresso powder or instant coffee for around 1–2 minutes, until smooth and slightly thickened.

6   Spread (or pipe) the coffee cream over the croissants, and finish with the nuts, if using.

Spiced Cherry & Ricotta Puff Pastry Tart

Serves 6–8

1 × 320g chilled all-butter
  puff pastry sheet
1 egg yolk, beaten
500g frozen dark
  sweet cherries
3 tbsp granulated sugar
2 tsp lemon juice
2 star anise
1 tsp cornflour, mixed with
  1 tbsp water
500g ricotta
4 tbsp icing sugar
2 tsp vanilla extract
1 small handful of pistachios,
  finely chopped (optional),
  to decorate

Cherry season in the UK is short, but frozen cherries mean you can enjoy this tart all year round. Dark cherries, in particular, hold up beautifully to spices. Here, they're simmered with star anise and sugar into a rich, glossy compôte, then spooned over golden puff pastry and a whipped vanilla ricotta that perfectly cuts through the sweetness. It's sharp, sweet, creamy and flaky all at once – and despite looking impressive, it couldn't be easier to make.

1 Heat your oven to 220°C/200°C fan.

2 Unroll the puff pastry on to a baking tray, using the paper the pastry comes in to line the tray. Score a 3cm border around the edge, then prick the centre all over with a fork. Brush the border with the beaten egg yolk. Bake for 12–15 minutes, or until golden brown and cooked through, then transfer it to a wire rack and leave to cool for 10 minutes.

3 While the puff pastry bakes, place the frozen cherries, granulated sugar, lemon juice and star anise in a small saucepan. Set the pan over a medium–high heat and bring the mixture to a simmer. Lower the heat to medium and cook for 10 minutes, stirring occasionally.

4 Stir in the cornflour slurry and cook for 30 seconds, or until thickened. Transfer the cherry compôte to a plate or shallow bowl and leave it to cool (more surface area = faster cooling).

5 In a medium mixing bowl, whisk the ricotta, icing sugar and vanilla until smooth, light and fluffy (around 1–2 minutes).

6 To assemble, spread the ricotta mixture over the cooled pastry, then spoon over the cherry compôte. Finish with the chopped pistachios, if using, and serve.

Cinnamon Date Pancakes

Makes 6–8 pancakes

4 soft Medjool dates, pitted
250ml whole milk (or milk
  of choice)
1 large egg
125g plain flour
½ tsp ground cinnamon
Pinch of salt
Butter (for best flavour) or
  vegetable oil (or any neutral
  oil), for cooking
Maple syrup or runny honey,
  to serve

One of the things I love most about creating recipes online is the constant exchange of ideas – learning from other creators and cultures, and the flavours they use. This recipe is inspired by *timir malawax*, a Somali date pancake I first discovered through @ilhanm.a. Made with blended dates, the pancakes are naturally sweet, beautifully spiced and land somewhere between a crêpe and a pancake – soft, slightly chewy and full of flavour. This is my version – they're rich, spiced with lots of cinnamon and best eaten warm with a drizzle of maple syrup.

*You can **make the batter in advance** – anywhere from 1 hour to overnight before you intend to eat. Just give it a good stir before cooking, as it may thicken slightly as it rests.*

1 Place the dates in a blender. Warm the milk in the microwave for 1 minute, or until warm, then pour it over the dates. Leave the mixture to sit for 5 minutes so the dates soften.

2 Crack in the egg, and add the flour, cinnamon and salt. Blitz to a smooth batter.

3 Heat a large non-stick frying pan over a medium heat and grease it very lightly with butter. Pour in a ladleful of the batter, swirling the pan to coat the base in a thin, even layer.

4 Cook the pancake for 1–2 minutes, or until the underside is golden and the edges start to crisp. Flip and cook the other side for another 30 seconds or so, or until speckled with brown spots.

5 Repeat with the remaining batter, keeping the pancakes warm in a low oven as you go. Serve them drizzled with maple syrup or honey.

Caramel Pineapple Ice Cream Sundaes

Serves 4

65g unsalted butter
1 small ripe pineapple, peeled,
   cored and cut into 8 wedges
100g dark brown soft sugar
2 × 7cm cinnamon sticks
4 big scoops good-quality
   vanilla ice cream
1 handful of toasted
   coconut flakes

This dessert is all about contrast – hot-cold, soft-crunchy, sweet-salty. You start by searing the pineapple until deeply golden and charred in places, then poach it in a cinnamon-spiced brown sugar syrup until beautifully tender. The sauce is finished with butter, whisked in to create a glossy, pineapple-infused salted caramel of sorts, ready to spoon over just before serving. Warm fruit, cold ice cream and a scattering of toasted coconut flakes – it's a big-flavour dessert that requires relatively little effort.

1 Set aside 25g of the butter, then cut the rest into 1cm-thick slices and refrigerate.

2 Melt the reserved 25g of butter in a large frying pan over a medium-high heat. Arrange the pineapple wedges in a snug single layer over the butter and cook undisturbed for 5–6 minutes, or until browned and charred in places. Flip and cook for another 3–5 minutes, or until browned.

3 Turn the heat down to medium, then add the sugar, cinnamon sticks, a pinch of salt and 4 tablespoons of water and give the pan a good shake. Cover the pan with a lid and cook the pineapple, flipping halfway through, for 8–10 minutes, or until tender (a skewer should slide through with little resistance).

4 Take the pan off the heat and transfer the wedges to bowls – you want two wedges per portion. Discard the cinnamon sticks.

5 Whisk the chilled butter into the sauce left in the pan until melted and emulsified. If the sauce feels too thin, return the pan to the heat and simmer for a couple of minutes until it has thickened slightly. Transfer to a bowl and leave it to cool a little.

6 To serve, add a big scoop of vanilla ice cream to each serving bowl, top with lots of the sauce and finish with a sprinkle of toasted coconut flakes.

Cheat's Lemon Pastéis de Nata

Makes 12

1 × 320g all-butter puff
  pastry sheet
85g caster sugar
1 lemon, zest, plus 1 tbsp juice
1 tbsp plain flour
150ml double cream
150ml whole milk
3 medium egg yolks (have
  them ready in a small bowl)

A *pastel de nata* is perhaps one of the world's best bakes – crisp, golden layers of buttery pastry filled with a luscious, just-set custard. However, to make one is incredibly labour-intensive. You need to laminate pastry, make a sugar syrup and bake it all at a screamingly high temperature. Unless you're a serious cook, it can be quite the undertaking. Cue these delicious cheats, with a bright, lemony twist. A sheet of puff pastry, rolled into a tight spiral and sliced, gives you a lovely flaky base, and the custard is quick to make, thickened just enough on the hob so that it bakes without splitting. They certainly aren't traditional, but they're very, very good.

Choose eggs that have a rich, golden yolk, which impart a beautiful yellow hue to the filling. I use Clarence Court Burford Brown eggs.

1 Heat your oven to 240°C/220°C fan.

2 Unroll the puff pastry, then roll it back up from the short end tightly into a log. Slice the log into 12 equal rounds – the spiral will give you the characteristic flaky edge. Place the rounds, cut-side down, in the holes of a non-stick muffin tin. Press each disc into the hollow and push it up the sides a little to create a shallow well. Chill until needed.

3 Place the sugar in a small saucepan. Add the lemon zest, then use your fingertips to rub the zest into the sugar for at least 30 seconds – this releases the lemons' essential oils, which will make the filling extra lemony and delicious.

4 Add the flour and salt and whisk to combine, then slowly pour in the double cream and milk, whisking until smooth. Set the saucepan over a medium heat and cook, stirring constantly, until the mixture thickens just enough to coat the back of a spoon (around 5 minutes).

5 Remove the saucepan from the heat and leave the custard to sit for 30 seconds. Whisk in the egg yolks, followed by the lemon juice. Strain the custard into a jug for a smooth finish, then pour it into the chilled pastry cases, filling each one about three-quarters full.

6 Bake for 15–18 minutes, or until puffed and golden with a few darker, caramelised spots on top. Cool the tarts in the tin for 5 minutes, then lift them out and transfer them to a wire rack to cool completely. They are best eaten on the day you make them.

Chai-Spiced Apple Crumble

Serves 4–6

For the filling
3 Bramley apples
  (around 550g)
½ lemon, juice
100g golden caster sugar
½ tbsp plain flour
1 tsp ground cinnamon
1 tsp ground ginger
¼ tsp ground cardamom
¼ tsp ground cloves
Custard, to serve (or cream or
  ice cream, if you really prefer)

For the topping
200g plain flour
150g golden caster sugar
150g very cold salted
  butter, cubed

Apple crumble is my favourite dessert. This version takes everything I love about it and dials it up with the warm, aromatic spices of a masala chai. It is very, very good – so good, in fact, that it's my favourite apple crumble recipe ever (a bold statement, I know). I hope it'll become a favourite of yours, too. Oh, and as an aside: in my book, serving this with anything other than custard would be borderline sacrilegious, but if you're a cream- or ice-cream-with-your-crumble kind of person, I won't judge (maybe just a little).

1 Heat your oven to 180°C/160°C fan. Peel, core and halve your apples, then cut them into 1cm-thick slices and transfer to a large mixing bowl.

2 Add the lemon juice, sugar, flour, cinnamon, ginger, cardamom and cloves and toss well to combine. Transfer the mixture to a 23cm cake tin and press it down lightly to stop too much of the topping from falling through the slices.

3 To make the topping, in a separate large mixing bowl, mix the 200g of flour and 150g of golden caster sugar, then add the cold butter and rub it in with your fingertips until the mixture looks like moist, coarse breadcrumbs. Scatter the crumble mixture evenly over the apples, but don't press it down.

4 Bake the crumble for 35–40 minutes, or until the topping is golden and crisp and the apples are bubbling underneath. The filling will be dangerously hot, so let the crumble cool for 10 minutes before serving. It's best served with custard, but single cream or ice cream wouldn't be a bad idea instead.

Mexican Hot Chocolate Brownies

Makes 16

50g cocoa powder
2 tsp ground cinnamon
½ tsp mild chilli powder
2 tsp vanilla extract
175g salted butter
3 large eggs
275g light brown soft sugar
75g caster sugar
100g plain flour
125g walnut halves and/or milk
  chocolate chips (optional
  but recommended)

The combination of chocolate, cinnamon and chilli just makes sense. These brownies are rich, fudgy and packed with deep cocoa flavour, with a subtle warmth that kicks in just after the first bite. The browned butter adds a toasty, nutty depth, while the mixture of sugars brings the perfect balance of chewiness and softness. The recipe says the walnuts are optional – but as far as I'm concerned, they're a must.

1 Place the cocoa powder, ground cinnamon, chilli powder and vanilla in a medium mixing bowl. Set aside.

2 Melt the butter in a medium saucepan set over a medium heat. It will bubble for a few minutes. As the bubbles die down, the milk solids will sink to the bottom and turn brown as they caramelise. This should take around 10 minutes.

3 Once the butter is golden brown and smells nice and nutty, pour it into the cocoa mixture, making sure to scrape in any browned bits from the bottom of the pan. Whisk until the cocoa is fully dissolved, then leave the mixture to cool for 10 minutes.

4 Meanwhile, heat your oven to 180°C/160°C fan. Line a 20cm × 20cm baking tin with baking paper.

5 Using an electric hand mixer on high speed, in a bowl whisk the eggs and both sugars until light, fluffy and pale in colour.

6 Using a rubber spatula, fold in the cooled cocoa-butter mixture, then sift and fold in the flour until there are no streaks of flour left. If you're adding walnuts and/or chocolate chips, fold them in at this stage.

7 Pour the batter into your prepared tin, spreading it evenly. Bake for 25–35 minutes, or until the edges are set and a knife inserted in the middle comes out with a bit of brownie batter clinging to it.

8 Let the brownies cool in the tin until completely cold, then slice them into 16 equal squares. They'll keep in an airtight container for up to two weeks or in the freezer for a month.

Earl Grey Baklava

Makes 24

300g granulated sugar
4 Earl Grey tea bags
½ lemon, juice
200g walnut halves
2 tbsp runny honey
¼ tsp fine sea salt
200g salted butter
14 sheets filo pastry

As all-time favourite desserts go, for me, baklava is right up there close to apple crumble (see page 205). If, though, you find it a *little* too sweet, this recipe is for you. It's all about balance. The syrup is infused with Earl Grey tea, which brings a soft, floral citrus note and just enough bitterness to offset the sweetness. Using salted butter further helps to round everything out, and browning it adds extra depth and flavour. It's a little labour-intensive, yes – but surprisingly simple once you get going, and *completely* worth the effort. It's the perfect dessert to make for a crowd – they'll be very impressed!

*Although it's not essential, I like to **make the syrup a day or two in advance** and store it covered in the fridge. Cold syrup poured over hot baklava gives the dessert the crispest finish, with an even soak that doesn't pool the syrup at the bottom of the pan.*

1 Start by making the syrup. Place the granulated sugar and 200ml of water in a small saucepan over a medium or medium–high heat. Bring the liquid to the boil, stirring to dissolve the sugar, then add the tea bags.

2 Lower the heat to medium and simmer until the syrup reaches 106°C. If you don't have a thermometer, look for a slight thickening – it should take around 10–12 minutes.

3 Discard the tea bags, then stir in the lemon juice. Transfer the syrup to a jug and leave it to cool completely.

4 Heat your oven to 170°C/150°C fan.

5 Blitz the walnuts in a food processor until finely chopped, then tip them into a mixing bowl. Add the honey and salt and mix well. The mixture should be a little sticky – this helps the nuts hold together, preventing them from scattering once you've added the syrup.

6 Melt the butter in a medium saucepan over a medium heat. Leave it to bubble for a few minutes, then the milk solids will sink to the bottom of the pan and begin to brown (this should take around 10 minutes).

continued overleaf . . .

7 Once the butter smells nutty and has gone from pale yellow to light brown, pour it into a bowl (if you leave it in the pan, it'll keep browning from the residual heat). Set the butter aside to cool slightly; the browned bits will settle at the bottom.

8 Trim the filo to fit a 30cm × 22cm tin. Brush the base and sides of the tin with a little of the brown butter, leaving behind the browned bits at the bottom of the bowl.

9 Lay 1 sheet of filo in the base of the tin and brush it with butter. Repeat with 4 more sheets, brushing each one as you go so that you have 5 buttered sheets in total.

10 Spread over half the walnut mixture, then top with another 4 sheets, again brushing each one with butter. Add the remaining nuts, then finish with a final layer of 5 buttered filo sheets.

11 Using a sharp knife, cut all the way through the pastry to form 24 diamonds, squares or triangles – whatever shape you prefer. Pour over any remaining butter, but leave the browned bits behind (they'll catch and burn in the oven).

12 Bake the baklava for 50 minutes to 1 hour 15 minutes, or until the top is golden and the bottom filo layers are fully cooked through. To test this, gently lift a piece from the centre of the tin and peek at the bottom. If it's not quite ready and the top is browning too quickly, loosely lay a piece of foil over the top.

13 As soon as the baklava comes out of the oven, pour over the cold syrup. It will bubble up. When the syrup stops bubbling, transfer the tin to a wire rack and leave the baklava to cool completely at room temperature, then separate the diamond shapes or squares and serve. This baklava will keep for several days, but it's at its absolute best within 24 hours of baking.

A Few Favourite Menu Ideas

Menu 1:
A Mexican-Inspired Affair

This menu is inspired by a recent trip to Mexico City, and more specifically a long lunch at the restaurant Contramar, which I still think about. The starter is my take on their iconic tuna tostadas – smoky, bold and unbelievably good. The main is a version of their red and green snapper, but I use salmon because it's easier to find. One side is rich and smoky, the other fresh and herby, and together they make a simple but striking centrepiece. Dessert keeps things in the same spirit: Mexican hot chocolate brownies that are deeply fudgy with a subtle warmth.

Smoky Tuna Tostadas
(page 109)

~

Red & Green Dinner Party Salmon
(page 68)

~

Mexican Hot Chocolate Brownies
(page 206)

Menu 2:
A Middle Eastern-Inspired Feast

This is my favourite way to feed people – a table full of colourful, vibrant dishes served family-style with plenty of warm flatbreads for scooping. This menu has something for everyone. The saffron lamb kebabs are rich, juicy and genuinely some of the most delicious kofta you'll ever try. The charred, deeply savoury mushrooms will convert even the most committed mushroom haters, and the smoky hispi cabbage has been a hit at every supper club I've ever hosted – even with cabbage sceptics! And for dessert: baklava with a twist.

Saffron Lamb Kebabs
(page 118)

~

Caramelised Mushroom Shawarma
(page 122)

~

Charred Hispi Cabbage with Cheat's Labneh
(page 128)

~

Earl Grey Baklava
(page 208)

Menu 3:
A Very Nigerian Spread

This menu feels like home to me – no starters, just hearty, deeply delicious food and a warm dessert to finish. My mum's chicken stew is the heart of it: rich, comforting and full of flavour. It's served with jollof rice, which needs no introduction. Everyone has their own way of making it, but my oven-baked version is foolproof. As for dessert, my family loves pineapple, so much so that my parents used to bring pineapples back from trips to Nigeria when I was younger (airport rules were less strict then!). It therefore feels only right to finish with my caramel pineapple ice cream sundaes – a nice contrast to the rice and stew.

Mum's Nigerian Chicken Stew
(page 156)

~

Oven-Baked Jollof Rice
(page 162)

~

Caramel Pineapple Ice Cream Sundaes
(page 201)

Menu 4:
A South Asian-Inspired Feast

This menu is inspired by some of my favourite South Asian flavours. It begins with the simplest but most satisfying starter: curry butter prawns, ready in under 10 minutes. For mains, there are three options: a fragrant lamb and spinach curry for the meat-lovers, an aromatic Sri Lankan-inspired crab curry for the pescatarians, or a rich, buttery red lentil dal for the vegetarians. Everything is served with rice and my viral tarka roasted cauliflower. And for dessert, chai-spiced apple crumble – a warm, fragrant favourite that I'm convinced will become your favourite too.

Curry Butter Prawns
(page 20)

~

Fragrant Lamb & Spinach Curry
(page 184)
or *Celebration Crab Curry*
(page 143)
or *Spiced Red Lentil Dal*
(page 179)

~

Tarka Roasted Cauliflower
(page 148)

~

Chai-Spiced Apple Crumble
(page 205)

Stockists and Sourcing

If you love Chinese food, there are a few ingredients that are, in my opinion, absolute must-haves for your pantry. They're long-lasting, endlessly versatile and feature in lots of the recipes in this book (and beyond!), so they definitely won't go to waste.

Online Stockists

Sous Chef

An independent, family-run company that hand-picks the best from global kitchens. Their range now spans more than 6,000 food products across over 20 cuisines – Japanese, Mexican, Italian, Korean, Chinese and beyond. They focus on quality, flavour-forward ingredients and deliver nationwide.

Oriental Mart

A long-standing, family-run online Asian super-market supplying more than 3,000 products – fresh, frozen and dried. They specialise in Chinese, Korean, Japanese, Thai, Malaysian, Filipino, Indonesian, Vietnamese and Singaporean ingredients, with nationwide delivery. Great for stocking up on noodles, sauces, pastes and frozen dumplings.

Oseyo & H Mart

Oseyo is the largest Asian supermarket retailer in the UK, with branches nationwide focused on Korean and wider Asian ingredients. For online orders, they deliver via H Mart, which carries a broad, Korean-led range, including store-cupboard staples, fresh produce and frozen goods. They also have a physical store in New Malden and deliver across the UK (excluding the Channel Islands).

Physical Shops

Middle Eastern & North African Grocers

In bigger UK cities, you'll often find large food halls specialising in Middle Eastern, Levantine and North African ingredients. Beyond these, the smaller Arabic, Turkish and Iranian corner shops are great for ingredients. They're often the best spots for bulk spices, good-value olive oils and high-quality tahini brands.

South Asian Grocers

Outside of the big supermarkets, your best bet for finding ingredients like fresh curry leaves, which feature in some of my favourite recipes in this book, is your local Indian, Pakistani or Sri Lankan grocer. Prices here are often lower, and stock moves fast, which means fresher herbs and spices. In London, they're very easy to find, particularly in Harrow, Wembley, Southall and East Ham. You'll find similar hubs in Birmingham, Leicester, Manchester, Bradford and other cities.

Index

About the Author

Zena Kamgaing is a London-based recipe developer and food creator known for her bold, flavour-driven cooking. She first came to public attention as a semi-finalist on Channel 4's *The Great Cookbook Challenge* with Jamie Oliver in 2022. She then went on to become a food creator for Mob Kitchen and has since built a community of over one million followers.

Zena's cooking is shaped by the food she grew up eating in her West African household in southwest London. Her vibrant, globally inspired recipes balance creativity with simplicity, proving that delicious food doesn't need to be complicated or time-consuming. She lives in London with her youngest sister.

Thank yous

This section is considered standard in any book, but as I sit here writing it, I find myself completely overcome with emotion (I'm full-on ugly crying). Writing a cookbook takes a village, and I'm grateful for so many people, so please bear with me as I give them their flowers.

First and foremost, thank you Jesus. It's a blessing to wake up and do what I love every day, and I don't take it for granted for a single moment.

To my Zena's Kitchen community, thank you for trusting me with your money and your groceries, and for giving my recipes a place in your homes. This book wouldn't exist without you. I'm deeply grateful for your support.

To my incredible mother, thank you for your unwavering support. You saw my passion for cooking from such a young age and nurtured it with so much love, and when I decided to turn it into a career, you were there – and continue to be there – every step of the way.

To my amazing father, thank you for being my rock. When I started this culinary journey, you didn't always understand what I was doing, but you supported me all the same, with so much love and patience. Without that support, I wouldn't be here, and I certainly wouldn't be writing this book.

To my wonderful sisters, Esther and Oluwadara – I don't say this nearly enough, but I love you so much. I've never actually said this out loud, but you're my best friends. Thank you for always being there, and for being my chief – and most honest – taste testers.

To the incredible Bloomsbury team, thank you. I couldn't have asked for a better publisher. Rowan Yapp, thank you for believing in me and this book, and for taking a chance on me. Lena Hall, thank you for your dedication and thoughtfulness, and for spearheading this entire process so smoothly. My deepest thanks to the wider Bloomsbury team: Mia Oakley, Laura Brodie, Isobel Turton, Marianne Laidlaw, Rose Brown, Danielle Rudasingwa and Lian Wilson. And across the pond: Ava Grandfield and Harriet LeFavour. I'm so grateful for the passion and excitement you've all put into this book.

To the superstar team that brought my recipes to life so beautifully, thank you. Yuki Sugiura, you're incredible. It's an honour to have you as the photographer for this book. Thank you for creating the most stunning photos – I will truly never get tired of looking at them.

Jennifer Kay, I couldn't have asked for a better prop stylist. I'll never forget walking into Yuki's studio on that first shoot day and seeing everything you'd gathered for just three days of shooting! Thank you for curating such beautiful dishes, backdrops and props that made every photo sing.

Emily Kydd, I'm in absolute awe of your food styling. Watching you work is so mesmerising – the detail, the placement, the plating – it's like seeing a painting take shape! Thank you for elevating my recipes to a level I could only have dreamed of. And Eden Owen-Jones (queen!) and Susannah Cohen (scrunchie icon!), thank you for your support throughout the shoots.

Luke Bird, thank you for the thought, creativity and care you've poured into designing this book. I know the hardest clients are the ones who don't really know what they want but still have strong opinions – and that was definitely me, haha. Yet with so little useful guidance from me, you created something so beautiful; it brought tears of joy to my eyes when I first saw it. I love absolutely everything you've done.

Judy Barratt and Caroline Stearns, thank you for your care and thoroughness with my words, and for being so patient with me when I wasn't always the best at staying on top of my inbox! I'm very grateful for you both.

To my beloved Fresh team, thank you. Debbie Catchpole, thank you for taking a chance on me all those years ago. You saw something in me long before I saw it in myself, and I'm so grateful for that. Tash Woffinden, thank you for giving me confidence at the very start of my journey, and for nurturing the belief that my value wasn't in the numbers – followers, engagement, any of it – but in the quality of my work. Verity O'Brien, Danielle Leith and Ellis Painter, thank you for all your hard work, for always having my back and for your endless patience.

To the wonderful foodie friends I've met along the way, thank you for your love, support and advice. There are more of you than I can list, but a special shoutout to Giuseppe Federici, Calum Harris, Bel Merid, Angelika Udenweze and Remi Idowu. And finally, to my former Mob colleagues, thank you for all the invaluable lessons. I'm not a trained chef, but Mob was, in many ways, a culinary and content university of sorts for me, and I'm grateful for everything I learned there.

Big love to you all! Zena x

BLOOMSBURY PUBLISHING
Bloomsbury Publishing Plc
50 Bedford Square, London, WC1B 3DP, UK
Bloomsbury Publishing Ireland Ltd
29 Earlsfort Terrace, Dublin 2, DO2 AY28, Ireland

BLOOMSBURY, BLOOMSBURY PUBLISHING and the Diana logo are trademarks of Bloomsbury Publishing Plc

First published in Great Britain, 2026

A catalogue record for this book is available from the British Library

ISBN: HB: 978-1-5266-9364-8; eBook: 978-1-5266-9363-1

10 9 8 7 6 5 4 3 2 1

Publisher: Rowan Yapp
Senior Editor: Lena Hall
Project Editor: Judy Barratt
Designer: Luke Bird
Photographer: Yuki Sugiura
Food Stylist: Emily Kydd
Prop Stylist: Jennifer Kay
Production: Laura Brodie

Printed and bound in China by C&C Offset Printing Co., Ltd

FSC
www.fsc.org

MIX
Paper | Supporting
responsible forestry
FSC® C008047

To find out more about our authors and books visit www.bloomsbury.com and sign up for our newsletters. For product safety related questions contact productsafety@bloomsbury.com